Culture in Special Education

Culture in Special Education

Building Reciprocal Family—Professional Relationships

by

Maya Kalyanpur, Ph.D.
Towson University
Maryland

and

Beth Harry, Ph.D.
University of Miami
Florida

·P A U L·H·
BROOKES
PUBLISHING Co.®

Baltimore • London • Sydney

Paul H. Brookes Publishing Co.
Post Office Box 10624
Baltimore, Maryland 21285-0624
www.brookespublishing.com

Typeset by Brushwood Graphics, Baltimore, Maryland.
Manufactured in the United States of America by
The Maple Press Co., York, Pennsylvania.

Second printing, March 2004.

Library of Congress Cataloging-in-Publication Data

Kalyanpur, Maya.
    Culture in special education : building reciprocal family–
professional relationships / by Maya Kalyanpur, Beth Harry.
      p.   cm
    Includes bibliographical references (p.) and index.
    ISBN 1-55766-376-9 (alk. paper)
    1. Special education—Social aspects—United States case studies.
2. Educational anthropology—United States case studies. 3. Special
education—Parent participation—United States case studies. I. Harry,
Beth. II. Title.
LC3969.K35   1999
371.9′04—dc21   99-26339
                                                                 CIP

British Library Cataloguing in Publication data are available from the
British Library.

Contents

v

123702

About the Authors

Maya Kalyanpur, Ph.D., Assistant Professor, Towson University, Department of Reading, Special Education and Technology, 409 Hawkins Hall, Towson, Maryland 21252-0001

Dr. Kalyanpur's scholarly interests have focused on teaching and research related to the needs and perspectives of families from culturally diverse backgrounds. In 1997, she received a postdoctoral fellowship at the Beach Center for Families and Disability at the University of Kansas at Lawrence, where the work documented in this book was carried out. She serves as a consulting editor for *Mental Retardation* and *Critical Inquiry into Curriculum and Instruction*. She was a classroom teacher and director of a private school for children with disabilities in New Delhi, India, before coming to the United States as a graduate student. She received her doctoral degree in special education from Syracuse University in 1994.

Beth Harry, Ph.D., Associate Professor, University of Miami, School of Education, Department of Teaching and Learning, Post Office Box 248065, Miami, Florida 33124-2040

Dr. Harry is a native of Jamaica and has lived and taught in Jamaica, Canada, Trinidad, and the United States. From a background in general education, Dr. Harry came into special education in response to the birth of her first child, Melanie, who had cerebral palsy. Prior to that, Dr. Harry taught elementary school in Jamaica; junior high school, high school, and community college in Toronto, Ontario, Canada; and in the School of Education at the University of the West Indies in Trinidad. After her daughter's birth, Dr. Harry founded and directed a private school for children with disabilities in Port of Spain, Trinidad. Dr. Harry came to the United States in 1985 and received her doctoral degree in special education from Syracuse University in 1989. Since then, she has focused on research and teaching related to the needs and perspectives of families from different ethnic backgrounds. Dr. Harry was an assistant professor of special education at the University of Maryland, College Park, from 1989 to 1995 and is Associate Professor in the Department of Teaching and Learning at the University of Miami, Florida.

Foreword

The historical separation of anthropology and psychology, whatever may have caused it, must surely be counted as one of the most stunting developments in the history of the human sciences. (Bruner, 1996, p. xiii)

No less than other fields, special education continues to struggle with the consequences of the historical separation of the foundational disciplines of anthropology and psychology. Among other factors since World War II, decolonization, the Civil Rights movement, and rising immigration have brought cultural issues into sharp focus. Every day in many schools, practitioners deal with a cultural diversity that might have always been there but only now is being recognized. As recognition grows, special education and its sister fields are undertaking journeys of discovery in search of a new and better way to take account of *culture,* both in concept and in practice. This is also the destination of two intrepid explorers of "culture in special education," Maya Kalyanpur and Beth Harry.

For Kalyanpur and Harry, culture is more complex, implicit, and subtle in its manifestations and effects than implied by the "surface differences" approach that dominates special education and other fields. Accordingly, they chose up-to-date maps to guide their journey that parallel those in anthropology that emphasize the evolution of culture over time in response to adaptive challenges (Edgerton, 1971, 1992; LeVine, 1977; Weisner, 1984). The results of this evolutionary process are beliefs and practices that help us adapt to persistent as well as changing circumstances. These beliefs and practices are organized as *cultural models* of how things work and what the proper ways are to survive and prosper (LeVine, 1977). Cultural models are social constructions of the world, widely shared by the members of a society, shaping their understanding of that world and their behavior in it (D'Andrade & Strauss, 1992). These models are so familiar and mundane that their functions and effects are often invisible to those for whom they are so important.

The impact of cultural models is everywhere: in daily routines in communities, homes, workplaces, play yards, and schools.

Everyone has a metaphorical storehouse of cultural models that can be changed, added to, and even ignored. As circumstances and environments change, these models are modified and changed as new challenges arise. The models are more plastic and less prescriptive than is implied by many discussions of culture. The cultural storehouse provides alternative models for dealing with adaptive challenges. Sometimes it contains models drawn from totally different ecological and cultural niches, which on the surface may seem contradictory but that provide adaptive responses to new circumstances (Roosens, 1994). For example, immigrants from rural Mexico to the urban United States blend their natal models with ones that they discover in their new communities (Goldenberg & Gallimore, 1995; Reese, Balzano, Gallimore, & Goldenberg, 1995). Many came to the United States for better economic opportunities for themselves and superior educational opportunities for their children. Although they themselves may not have attended school or had parents who pushed education, they quickly adopt the U.S. cultural model of schooling as a means of upward social mobility, including the aspiration that their children attend college and have a professional career. To adapt in U.S. cities and implement the U.S. schooling and mobility model, immigrants may rely on traditional Mexican values of family unity, respect and interdependence, parental authority, kinship networks, and related adaptive tools. Thus, the agrarian cultural model in Latin American countries is for newly arrived immigrants to the United States "a continuous source of meaning and guidance" (LeVine & White, 1986) even as they implement a new schooling and social mobility model.

Values and practices encoded in cultural models are not necessarily internally consistent or consistently related to behavior (Strauss, 1992). This seeming "irrationality" can be understood as preparation for shifting challenges, for which different cultural models may be required. A model that may contradict another can provide an alternative response to changing circumstances. In the cultural storehouse are a variety of adaptive tools, left largely unused perhaps for a few generations but familiar and socially acceptable if need arises. Not all models must be enacted even if endorsed. Some features of cultural models have motivating properties, including elements with moral or quasi-moral force sufficient that an individual feels an obligation to carry out in behavior. But other elements of a model, perhaps strongly endorsed in the abstract, are *not* acted on or *do not* have directive force for every individual.

This variability in model enactment means that culture is not a nominal variable to be attached equally to every individual like a "social" address, in the same way that age, height, or gender might be. Treating culture in this way assumes that everyone who claims membership in or is assigned to a group has common natal experiences and acts on available cultural models in a uniform, unvarying fashion. In many cases, they do not. *Assuming homogeneity of experience and behavior of individuals within cultures, without empirical evidence, is unwarranted* (Pelto & Pelto, 1978; Whiting, 1976; Whiting & Whiting, 1975). A parallel error is to treat national or ethnic status as equivalent to a common cultural experience for individuals (Phinney, 1996).

This brings us to a key challenge that Kalyanpur and Harry present to the field of special education: Special education, they argue, must shake itself loose from the socially mischievous habit of defining culture as a *trait* and assigning it to all individuals in a group defined by a superficial analysis of social address such as family structure, ethnicity, or socioeconomic status (Bronfenbrenner, 1986). Stereotyping is the probable consequence, they argue, of treating as alike everyone with a similar social address. In schools, this error takes the form, for example, of placing children in programs based on superficial social address and prevailing stereotypes rather than on true understanding of cultural models in the lives of individuals.

Kalyanpur and Harry are not offering special education an easy road to better understanding of culture. For them, learning about culture is a permanent journey of discovery, something to be learned from firsthand contacts with people from different places. Their advice is *do not assume* based on surface assessment, and *do take a "posture of cultural reciprocity"* to inquire and learn about individuals' cultural models. Do not make assumptions about individuals based on ethnicity, gender, social class, and other such proxies. Assuming, they assert, can get you into a lot of trouble. Special educators are urged to ask "why" and "what does it mean" that a family has differing views of potentially conflicted topics such as child abuse, the meaning of work, and the value of independence versus continuing family dependence. What might seem at first appraisal a fundamentally different view of child abuse, for example, should spur a special educator to deeper inquiry rather than an offhand and facile conclusion. As far as we know, virtually every society has a model of child welfare and development that distinguishes benign from abusive treatment (Weisner, 1984). Yet exactly where benign ends and abuse begins will vary, creating the possibility of contested definitions. It is just such issues that demand a more sophisticated concept of culture, one that gets at the implicit and the subtle, avoids stereotyping by social address, and urges examination of one's own cultural models of belief and practice. Some of their views sharply challenge conventional views and practice, but these two explorers wisely urge their special education colleagues to take a permanent journey of discovery—a constant search for a more sophisticated and sensitive understanding of how culture plays out in their own and in their clients' personal and professional models of reality.

Accommodating to culture certainly and clearly involves sensitivity to differences, a recognition that is happily and at long last dawning in many professional fields. As this good thing proceeds, it is vital to remember that cultural accommodation cuts both ways—making changes if needed but recognizing similarities when they exist rather than searching only for features that distinguish one group from others. To ignore either differences or similarities is not in the best interest of children, families, and communities. As they confront the challenges posed by an increasingly diverse society, special educators certainly need to be sensitive to cultural differences. But knowing what we all share is just as important as recognizing how we differ (Goldenberg & Gallimore, 1995).

Ronald Gallimore, Ph.D.
Professor
Department of Psychiatry & Biobehavioral Sciences
and Graduate School of Education & Information Studies
University of California–Los Angeles

REFERENCES

Bronfenbrenner, U. (1986). Ecology of the family as a context for human development. *Developmental Psychology, 22*, 723–742.

Bruner, J. (1996). Foreword. In B. Shore, *Culture in mind: Cognition, culture, and the problem of meaning* (p. xiii). Oxford: Oxford University Press.

D'Andrade, R.G., & Strauss, C. (Eds.). (1992). *Human motives and cultural models.* Cambridge, NY: Cambridge University Press.

Edgerton, R.B. (1971). *The individual in cultural adaptation: A study of four East African peoples.* Berkeley: University of California Press.

Edgerton, R.B. (1992). *Sick societies: Challenging the myth of primitive harmony.* New York: Free Press.

Goldenberg, C.N., & Gallimore, R. (1995). Immigrant Latino parents' values and beliefs about their children's education: Continuities and discontinuities across cultures and generations. In P. Pintrich & M. Maehr (Eds.),

Advances in motivation and achievement (Vol. 9, pp. 183–227). Greenwich, CT: JAI Press.

LeVine, R. (1977). Child rearing as cultural adaptation. In P. Leiderman, S. Tulkin, & A. Rosenfeld (Eds.), *Culture and infancy* (pp. 15–27). New York: Academic Press.

LeVine, R., & White, M. (1986). *Human conditions: The cultural basis of educational development.* New York: Routledge & Kegan Paul.

Pelto, P.J., & Pelto, G.H. (1978). *Anthropological research: The structure of inquiry.* Cambridge, NY: Cambridge University Press.

Phinney, J.S. (1996). When we talk about American ethnic groups, what do we mean? *American Psychologist, 51*(9), 918–927.

Reese, L., Balzano, S., Gallimore, R., & Goldenberg, C. (1995). The concept of *educación*: Latino family values and American schooling. *International Journal of Educational Research, 23*(1), 57–81.

Roosens, E. (1994, November 3–5). *Education for living in pluriethnic societies.* Paper presented at Carnegie/Jacobs Foundation Conference Frontiers in the Education of Young Adolescents, Marbach Castle, Germany.

Strauss, C. (1992). What makes Tony run? Schemas as motives reconsidered. In R.G. D'Andrade & C. Strauss (Eds.), *Human motives and cultural models* (pp. 197–224). Cambridge, NY: Cambridge University Press.

Weisner, T.S. (1984). Ecocultural niches of middle childhood: A cross-cultural perspective. In W.A. Collins (Ed.), *Development during middle childhood: The years from six to twelve* (pp. 335–369). Washington, DC: National Academy of Sciences Press.

Whiting, B.B. (1976). Unpackaging variables. In K.F. Riegel & J.A. Meacham (Eds.), *The changing individual in a changing world* (pp. 303–309). Chicago: Aldine.

Whiting, B., & Whiting, J. (1975). *Children of six cultures.* Cambridge, MA: Harvard University Press.

Preface

The idea for this book began many years ago when Beth and I were fellow doctoral students at Syracuse University. For a course on qualitative research methods, we were required to conduct independently a qualitative study on a topic of our choice and write up our analysis of the findings. Having come from India, I was interested in the issue of transfer of technology, or how special education strategies and models that are successful in Western countries often are unsuitable when applied in developing countries with different social, political, economic, and cultural contexts, and wondered whether the same problem occurred on a smaller scale in the United States, affecting families from culturally diverse groups. Toward this purpose, I interviewed disability-related service providers and Native American families of children with disabilities on a reservation and found indeed that the services offered frequently were based on recommended practices and models that were successful in the mainstream and were not suited to the culturally variant child-rearing beliefs and practices of the Native American mothers. However, because I had expected to find evidence of this unsuitability, I thought my idea hardly novel and my analysis somehow incomplete. So I gave Beth, a fellow "cultural variant" from Jamaica who also had studied the perspectives of culturally diverse families, a copy of my paper to read.

The next day, she came up to me, excited. Turning quickly to a page in my paper, she read a sentence aloud: "If we assume that special education services are defined by the underlying values and social practices of a people, then we can identify the culture-bound constructs that have determined these services." She looked up at me and said, "But you're assuming that we *would* assume this. I think the problem is that we don't. You see, the professionals in your study weren't making this assumption. That's why they took what worked here and applied it there and nobody questioned it."

Now it was my turn to become excited. "Of course, I'm making assumptions myself! That's the missing piece. It's because we *do not* realize that special education comes from the culture that we assume that it means the same everywhere." It was the beginning of many such conversations on what was to become what Beth called "our favorite topic." Over the years, we pondered and discussed the idea further until we knew that we had enough to fill a book. And the more we researched the problems of culturally diverse families of children with disabilities and presented our ideas to professionals at workshops and conferences, the more we became convinced of the need for such a book.

During these years, we noticed that the field of special education was making vigorous efforts to respond to the demographic changes occurring among the families and children with disabilities served. Policy makers, practitioners, and academics alike argued the need for nondiscriminatory assessment toward ameliorating the problem of overrepresentation of culturally and linguistically diverse students in special education as well as the need for cultural competence toward facilitating the participation of these students' families in the education decision-making process. These efforts have helped create an awareness of some of the problems that culturally diverse students and their families face and, in many cases, have led to the development of various strategies toward resolving these problems. The 1997 reauthorization of and amendments to the Individuals with Disabilities Education Act (IDEA; PL 105-17) further reinforce this point:

> The education of children with disabilities can be made more effective by strengthening the role of parents and ensuring that families of such children have meaningful opportunities to participate in the education of their children at school and at home.... There is a need in each state for a comprehensive, coordinated interagency system of family support for families of children with disabilities that is family centered, family directed, and culturally competent. (20 U.S.C. Chapter 33)

Yet the participation of families from culturally diverse and socioeconomically disadvantaged backgrounds in shared decision making continues to be low. Why, we must ask, is the ideal of collaboration between professionals and parents from culturally diverse backgrounds so elusive? Is it because professionals lack understanding of families' cultural values and beliefs? We think that this is only part of the picture, for if that were the case, then the plethora of information about the cultural orientations and belief systems of different cultural groups generated in the past few years should have created awareness and understanding enough. Perhaps culture itself is our culprit for, as Hall wrote,

Culture is man's medium; there is not one aspect of human life that is not touched and altered by culture. This means personality, how people express themselves (including shows of emotion), the way they think, how they move, how problems are solved, how their cities are planned and laid out, how transportation systems function and are organized, as well as how economic and government systems are put together and function. However, it is frequently the most obvious and taken-for-granted and therefore the least studied aspects of culture that influence behavior in the deepest and most subtle ways. (1981, pp. 16–17)

We expect professionals and parents to collaborate in the midst of something so highly nuanced and taken for granted as culture. Moreover, although as professionals we know, even expect, that the families' values will be different, we often forget to ask, "Different from what?" For we, too, bring our culture, the culture of special education, to the interaction.

Collaboration between professionals and parents from culturally diverse backgrounds, then, requires *reciprocal understanding* of taken-for-granted beliefs. When families do not understand the culture of professionals, then for collaboration to occur, we must expect to explain our special education culture to families and create a shared understanding. The crux of the issue, however, is that often we ourselves may not be aware of these values and assumptions that are embedded in special education policy and practice. In other words, it is because we *do not* realize that special education comes from the culture that we assume that it would mean the same to all families everywhere.

By identifying the cultural values and assumptions that are embedded in special education policy and practice in the United States, this book is intended to help professionals in special education and other related fields who, in the course of their professional practice, are and will be collaborating with families from culturally diverse backgrounds. Indeed, with the changing demographics, more and more of us will face this challenge. When we recognize the values behind our own practice, we become more open and responsive to the values of the families whom we serve. This knowledge empowers us, and, as we communicate this knowledge to families in our collaboration, it empowers families in turn. And our children will reap the benefits.

REFERENCES

Hall, E.T. (1981). *Beyond culture*. Garden City, NY: Anchor Press/Doubleday.
Individuals with Disabilities Education Act (IDEA) Amendments of 1997, PL 105-17, 20 U.S.C. §§ 1400 *et seq.*

Acknowledgments

I thank Professors Ann Turnbull and Rud Turnbull at the Beach Center for Families and Disability, University of Kansas, for offering me a postdoctoral fellowship at the Beach Center that enabled me to write this book; for their helpful comments on early drafts of Chapters 4 and 2, respectively; and, above all, for their unstinting generosity, support, and thoughtfulness. I also thank Dean Dennis Hinkle at the School of Education, Towson University, for demonstrating his faith in me by instantly endorsing my decision to accept the offer of the fellowship.

My thanks also go to my friends and colleagues at the Beach Center for the many ways in which they helped the process of writing: Ben Furnish gave both editorial feedback and invaluable assistance with the bibliography; Vicki Turbiville, Mike Ruef, Betsy Santelli, Amanda Reichard, Anne Guthrie, and Denise Poston gave well-considered feedback on Chapter 4; Maren Santelli and Patricia Grossi helped obtain the readings for the book; Steve Pollard responded promptly to any computer foul-ups; and Lois Weldon and Richard Viloria helped make the transition from Maryland to Kansas smooth. A special thanks to Martha Blue-Banning, whose warmth, support, and gentle humor helped me keep things in the right perspective. My appreciation goes to Lisa Benson, Acquisitions Editor, and Christa Horan, Book Production Editor, at Brookes Publishing for their patience, persistence, and understanding.

I am grateful to Sona Gollerkeri, Chikako Thomsen, Joe O'Brien, and Jeanine Thurmaier for their friendship and for helping out with child care, sometimes on very short notice. To my faith keepers, my husband, Vijay Rao, and my parents, Leela Rao and Bhaskar Kalyanpurkar, for traveling hundreds of miles to lend their support, many, many thanks. Finally, I am indebted to my son, David Rao, then 5, who, in his words, "left America" to come to Kansas with me on the strength of his mother's promise and her dream.

Maya Kalyanpur

I thank my husband, Bernard Telson, for his interest in this project over the years. His many personal anecdotes enriched Maya's and my thinking on the topic of cultural reciprocity.

Beth Harry

We dedicate this book to Marsha Smith-Lewis, dear friend and colleague, who passed away in December 1993. Marsha was an integral participant in our initial conceptualizations and a fellow presenter in our first public presentation on the posture of cultural reciprocity at the 1992 conference of the National Association of Multicultural Education in Orlando, Florida. The following poem was written by Beth and read at Marsha's funeral.

marsha

now we know why you lived the way you did
      never saving today's joy for tomorrow's promise
      never saying "no" for fear of should and ought and maybe
      never saying "I can't" just because it looked too hard
      hard-headed, headstrong, no one could tell you what to do
      because you'd figured it all out and would take your chances
      right or wrong

now we know why you loved the way you did
      fiercely loyal once your spirit took to someone
      that's my friend—don't mess with her
      that's my family—I'll do anything for them
      that's my man—I'll fuss with him all I want
      but don't you put your mouth in it

now we know why you worked the way you did
      always committed to a purpose you believed in
      always clear about the right or wrong of things
      no patience with the academic fluff that went against
      all you knew about being Black in America

now we know why you wouldn't say "I'm dying"
      because to say so might have made it happen sooner
      might have robbed you of the chance to say "yes"
      just one more time
      might have robbed us of one more of your smiles
      or might have dulled our memory of your laughter

now we know that you were the way you were
      because you had so much to give
      and so little time to give it
      so much to share
      and so many to share it with
      because we had so much to learn from you
      and so little time to learn it

marsha
      your feet were always on the ground
      but your spirit soared beyond most people's dreams
      no bushel holding back your light

now you have wings

Cultural Underpinnings of Special Education

Beth's Story

On a trip to Albuquerque in the middle of winter, I had the disconcerting experience of boarding a plane at the Baltimore/Washington
International Airport and, within minutes, being asked to deplane.
Back at the departure gate, I waited with other anxious passengers
for some information regarding the status of the flight. After about a
half an hour's wait came the following announcement: "Passengers
on the flight to Albuquerque, please be advised that we will be
boarding in about an hour's time, since a new piece of equipment
will soon be arriving from Philadelphia."

Being a very phobic air traveler and knowing nothing about the
mechanics of any kind of vehicle, I reacted to this announcement
with some consternation. I thought, "A new piece of equipment?
What could it be? A wrench? A new steering wheel? Some new
radar equipment? Does this mean that we'll have to wait while they
fix it or replace some part? Shouldn't they just give us a new plane?"
I went to the desk and asked the attendant what the announcement
meant. The reply was, "It said they're sending a new plane."

This was about 4 years ago, and I still remember vividly my annoyance at what seemed to me the use of language as a subterfuge.
Since then, I have repeated this story to many people, asking their

---

Throughout this book, the authors introduce each chapter with a personal anecdote that highlights the impact that unstated cultural assumptions can have on people who do not share those assumptions. Both authors
of the book take turns telling their stories.

impression of the meaning of this language event. Everyone agrees that it is a prime example of jargon, in which a group of people who belong to a particular field of work use language in a way that differs from the way that it would be used by the population at large. It also is an example of how people use jargon that is specific to their field without even being aware that they are doing so.

My main concern is the effect that such language might have on the uninitiated. This depends on the perspective that any individual has regarding airplane travel. For me, connotations for the word *equipment* as compared with *airplane* reflect my fear of flying; thus, the following associations with equipment come to mind readily: a tool, a large class of technical items, something neutral, something made and manipulated by human beings. Associations for *airplane* rush in just as quickly: something that takes you up into the sky, defying the laws of gravity; something huge and powerful that carries large numbers of people at once; something that can come crashing down to Earth and kill those large numbers of people. Thus, to refer to an airplane as a "piece of equipment" is to minimize, neutralize, and mitigate the features that, for me, are dominant: its power and its danger. A piece of equipment is, after all, within human control—simply a tool at our disposal—whereas an airplane in its totality seems, somehow, more than the sum of its parts. Someone who finds flying safe and exhilarating might have interpreted this kind of communication quite differently. My point is that language is more than denotative: It is connotative, and connotations evoke emotions that are beyond rationalization.

In the departure lounge at the Baltimore/Washington International Airport, the language of the announcement reflected a technological culture with which the airplane experts probably identified. Within that culture, such use of the word *equipment* is probably commonplace and not thought of as having any particular effect. As an anxious passenger, however, I was a total outsider to that culture.

In much the same way, we, the authors of this book, came as outsiders to the culture of special education in the United States. We had not, of course, expected to see it in that way. In our home countries, Jamaica and India, we had assumed that disabilities were factual phenomena and that specialized education for people with disabilities would, somehow, reflect a universality of meaning, of affect, or, at the very least, of value. That is not to say that we thought that we already knew the answers or even all of the questions. Certainly, we expected to be introduced to new theories and new instructional approaches, but neither of us had conceived of the coming experience as a cultural event, the underpinnings of which would take several years for us to "unpack."

CULTURAL IDENTITY AND THE ACCULTURATION PROCESS

What do we mean by the "culture of special education"? In its larger meaning, the term *culture* denotes the shared implicit and explicit rules and traditions that express the beliefs, values, and goals of a group of people. Let us consider, first, the meaning of cultural identity.

Children are raised within a cultural framework that imposes rewards and sanctions for efficient learning of the group's norms and expectations. According to the traditional view of culture, most individuals have been brought up within one such framework, and the process of acculturation involves being introduced to a new system and gradually accommodating to it. Thus, at a given point in time, one's acculturation might be at any point on a spectrum, such as that described by Ramírez and Castañeda (1974), who identified three points—traditional, dualistic, and atraditional—or Leung's (1988) framework, which specified "marginality" as the transition between traditionalism and biculturalism and conceived of the fourth stage as "overacculturation," whereby the traditional elements have been totally rejected. To this, Red Horse (1988) added a fifth stage, which he called "pan-renaissance," in which a group seeks a revitalization or revival of the traditional culture, such as that sought by African Americans in the 1960s or by some North American Indian tribes in the United States and Canada.

The foregoing "stage" theories suggest that cultures are somehow discrete, that acculturation is a process of change over time, and that an individual can be no more than "bicultural"—a state that is often metaphorically described as "walking in two worlds" (Henze & Vanett, 1993, p. 116). A further implication that is based on historical analysis is that the individual who does not belong to the dominant group is expected to undergo this process of acculturation. Wright, Saleeby, Watts, and Lecca (1983), taking a similar theoretical stance, addressed three views of how cultural groups might interact in a multicultural society. These theorists examined both the pluralistic model and the assimilation model and proposed, instead, a goal of "cultural integration." According to Wright et al., the pluralistic model is represented by the metaphor of the "mosaic," which suggests that cultural groups remain separate but mutually respecting; they argued that this continues to encourage groups to remain separate and may actually promote mutual stereotyping rather than understanding. The assimilation model, by contrast, is represented by the metaphor of the melting pot, which Wright et al. saw as culture killing in that key features of a culture are transformed through the process of blending with others. Rather than either of these two models, then, Wright et al. recommended "cultural integration," which would be accomplished through cultural exchange and mutual influence.

In contrast to the foregoing traditional views of cultural groups as manifesting definite boundaries that give way through acculturation, Banks (1997a, 1997b) suggested a more fluid and less discrete way of thinking about cultural identity. Banks's theory is applicable to multicultural societies such as the United States, in which there is a "national culture as well as ethnic and other subsocieties and institutions" (1997b, p. 6). Banks described a complex picture of macro and micro levels of culture, whereby the macrocultural framework is an overarching national frame that includes many microcultural groups, each of which participates to varying extents in the macro culture, while simultaneously retaining varying amounts of its original cultural traditions. Thus, the cultural identity of any individual may reflect features of the macroculture, of one's original microculture, and of any other microcultural groups within the society. Factors such as race, ethnicity, nationality, language, social status, and geographical location are key ingredients in the pattern of identity that emerges.

Furthermore, individuals may develop affiliations with professional or personal interest groups that have their own norms and rules, and these features also feed into cultural identity. As Banks (1997a, 1997b) noted, each individual belongs to several groups at the same time and may experience stronger or weaker identification with the tenets of one group as compared with another, based on the extent of socialization that is experienced within each group. It is also interesting to note that a "group" may be explicitly identified as such by means of well-defined beliefs and practices, such as a religion, but it also may be a group by virtue of some particular experience, such as being the parent of a child with a disability. Cultural identity, then, is multifaceted and highly individualized.

Both of us can readily cite affiliations with several microcultural groups, while simultaneously participating in the American macroculture. These affiliations are strong enough to require sometimes separate, sometimes overlapping, and sometimes conflicting sets of rules for conduct. Both of us identify with the academic community, with women, and with other parents; in particular, I feel affiliated to others who have children with disabilities. My primary ethnic affiliation is Caribbean and also Black in a broader sense, whereas Maya identifies herself as Indian and Hindu.

SPECIAL EDUCATION
AS A CULTURAL INSTITUTION

What does it mean, then, to say that an individual shares membership in the culture of special education? Let us begin by viewing the special education system as a subsystem within the social institution of education. Bullivant (1993) explained the powerful relationship between the larger, or macro, culture and the social institutions that carry out the cultural program of a society. First, he identified such institutions as "major interrelated systems of social roles and norms (rules) organized to satisfy important social and human needs" (p. 31). These include the nuclear family, the education system, the legal system, and so forth. Bullivant explained that

> The distinctive pattern or style of an institutional agency's operation is determined by its charter or ideology. A charter consists of a collection of beliefs, values, and ideas about what the institutional agency aims at (its ends) and how it will arrange its structure and organization (the means) to carry out its aims. . . . (p. 32)
>
> Much as a computer is programmed by software containing instructions, so an institutional agency's ideology, organization, structure, and operation are programmed by instructions and information that enable it to function properly. They also provide people in the agency with the necessary knowledge and ideas about what behaviors are appropriate and what are not, together with the rules and routines to follow. All these instructions, knowledge, and information are selected from the society's culture. (p. 33)

According to this analysis of social institutions, we can expect that the special education system will reflect the "beliefs, values, and ideas" regarding both the ends and the means of education, which, in turn, reflect those of the national macroculture.

Several powerful analyses of the historical development of U.S. public schools have emphasized that the education system's main charge has been transmission of the essential cultural tenets of U.S. society. Indeed, Spindler and Spindler (1990) asserted that all American cultural dialogue, whether it be public speech, such as editorials, public policy, campaign speeches, and classroom discussions, or private speech, such as parent–child interactions, is facilitated by a tacit understanding of "core" American values. They identified five such core values:

Freedom of speech (and other forms of personal freedom); the rights of
an individual (to be an individual and act in his or her own behalf);
equality (as equality of opportunity and including sexual equality); the
desirability of achievement attained by hard work (and the belief that
anyone can achieve success if he or she works hard enough); and social
mobility (the assumption that anyone can improve social status because the social structure is open and hard work will get you there.
(p. 23)

Similarly, Tyack and Hansot (1982) placed the Protestant ethic and
capitalism at the core of the history of public schooling in America.
These authors described the early 19th-century efforts to establish a
common school system as a "crusade" whose charge was to combine the Christian virtues of a "generalized Protestantism," such as
hard work, literacy, temperance, and frugality, with "a work ethic
and ideology favoring the development of capitalism" (Tyack &
Hansot, 1982, p. 28). Along with this was the ideal of equity, one of
the cornerstones of American democracy.

The latter half of the 19th century saw two powerful movements that further influenced the direction of the public school vision: First, industrialization, as a result of which the vision became
increasingly secular and, driven by a growing faith in science and
scientific management, incorporated the Protestant ethic into what
Tyack and Hansot referred to as "the gospel of efficiency" (1982,
p. 121). The second force directing the charge of education was the
vastly increasing and changing nature of the immigrant population.
Concerns about the socialization of non–Anglo-Saxon immigrants
resulted in the drive to "Americanization," which, by the 1930s and
1940s, was considered essential to combat the evils of urbanization,
poverty, and cultural differences that were consistently interpreted
as deficits of character and capability (Fass, 1989). As many scholars have shown (e.g., Fass, 1989; Gould, 1981), beliefs about cultural and racial inferiority were fueled by the development of "mental testing" and were applied both to immigrants and to native-born
minorities.

This issue brings us to the relation between the general education and special education systems. As Fass (1989) and Skrtic
(1991) pointed out, equity is a difficult goal to achieve because of a
conflict between the rapidly increasing heterogeneity of the school
population and the drive for a bureaucratic uniformity in schools.
As school leaders turned more and more to the IQ test as a means of
sorting students into the manageable units required by the gospel of
efficiency, the concept of individual deficit became institutional-
ized. This was the cornerstone on which the special education sys-

tem was built, and the fact that this system still serves a dispropor-
tionately high percentage of minorities ought not be surprising. Indeed, Skrtic described special education as "the institutional practice that emerged in the 20th century to contain the failure of public
education to realize its democratic ideals" (1991, p. 46).

Beyond a historical analysis, structural analysis also reveals
the cultural charge given to the institution of education. Skrtic
(1991) offered a detailed explication of how the epistemological
and organizational bases of general education became interpreted
and incorporated into the professional culture of special education.
In essence, he argued that the field of education has been dominated by the positivist tradition of knowledge, which, with its assumption that reality is objective and unchangeable, has led to a
mechanistic model of services ("a machine bureaucracy") and to a
view of teaching that is based on a model of technical rationality
(see also Schön, 1983). Special education, Skrtic argued, has been
expressed as a "more extreme version" (1991, p. 105) of that model,
and the special education teacher, "even more so than the general
education teacher, is conceptualized as a technician" (1991,
p. 106).

Hall (1981) asserted that this emphasis on objectivity occurs
most frequently in what he termed "low context" cultures, in which
"bureaucratic ranking systems" are based on the belief that when
both action and agent are stripped of their contexts, or "decontextualized," the action can be conducted by anyone anywhere and, conversely, still have the same meaning in all contexts. He gave the example of the American legal system, which in allowing "only
established facts, stripped of all contexting background data, as ad-
missible as evidence" is, he stated, "the epitome of low-context systems" (Hall, 1981, p. 107). Special education law, in its requirement
for categorical classification of children's disabilities, reflects exactly this kind of abstracted, low-context language. Conversely,
"high context" cultures would accept, even encourage, conclusions
that tolerate greater ambiguity.

According to Skrtic (1995b), the low-context culture of technical rationalism results in an uncritical approach to the underpinnings of special education. Skrtic's answer to this is "critical pragmatism," which

> Approaches decision making in a way that recognizes and treats as
> problematic the assumptions, theories, and metatheories behind pro-
> fessional models, practices, and tools; it accepts the fact that our as-
> sumptions, theories, and metatheories themselves require evaluation
> and reappraisal. (1995b, p. 44)

FOCUS OF THIS BOOK

In this book, epistemological and organizational aspects of professional culture as they relate to parent–professional relationships and Skrtic's point about an uncritical approach are essential to our own arguments. We use a critical pragmatist approach to examine the underpinnings that form the value base of special education—in particular, the core American values of equity, individualism, personal choice, and hard work (Spindler & Spindler, 1990). Furthermore, we place our concern within the context of the inevitably multicultural nature of the United States and the challenge that special education professionals face in collaborating with families and individuals whose implicit and explicit value base may be radically different from their own. Thus, the bulk of the book addresses the issue of how the ideals of the U.S. macroculture are represented in special education and the resulting implications for cross-cultural communication.

At this point, however, it is important for us to specify the book's central argument: Professional knowledge is largely acquired by an implicit process that needs to be made explicit and conscious if school personnel are to become effective collaborators in a multicultural society. Critical pragmatism makes that process explicit (Skrtic, 1995a). Our "posture of cultural reciprocity" (discussed in Chapter 5) facilitates professionals' engagement in this process to bring about effective parent–professional collaboration.

BECOMING A MEMBER:
THE IMPORTANCE OF EMBEDDED BELIEFS

How does an individual gain membership in the institution of special education? First, each individual brings his or her own complex of macro- and microcultural frameworks and the belief systems that they espouse. The process that prepares the individual for membership in this particular institution, however, draws most heavily on the macrocultural belief systems on which the field is built. Because most professionals who come into this field have demonstrated through their success in the education system considerable mastery of the belief systems of the overarching macroculture, it is clear that the implicit and explicit beliefs of the macroculture are not new to them. Induction into special education, then, is accomplished by building on the implicit knowledge base of the macroculture through formal instruction in the theoretical and applied knowledge of the field and, finally, through practical experience in schools (Skrtic, 1991).

Our central point is that new members often learn the approved goals—and means of attaining those goals—without having to specify explicitly their cultural basis. In most situations, the rules of a cultural institution may never be taught explicitly to the inductee precisely because the insiders themselves may not be aware of the rules. Indeed, theorists have argued that the teaching of social and economic norms and expectations to students in school is a covert or tacit process (Apple & Beane, 1995; Giroux, 1993; Greene, 1988). As indicated previously, through the cultural hegemony established by the dominant group, the microculture of public schools in America reflects the values of the macroculture. Some scholars assert that although teachers are perceived to be competent when they successfully socialize their students into the "nonacademic but educationally significant consequences of schooling" (Vallance, 1983, p. 9), they rarely are aware of their role in the process of what Bowles and Gintis (1976) called "cultural reproduction." In other words, to the teachers, insiders themselves, these nonacademic aspects of learning rarely are an explicit part of the pedagogical process.

Illich (1971) stated that the disempowerment, or the "deskilling," of teachers leaves them with little choice but to perpetuate this indoctrination. For instance, individuals who undergo professional training to become teachers are required to learn the pedagogy of "classroom management" toward inculcating certain desired student behaviors such as obedience and participation, which are perceived to be valued and useful skills for adult life in an industrial society. The only choice that they have is how they might teach these behaviors.

This kind of professional preparation appears to have two unfortunate consequences: First, the fact that school professionals are not made aware of the cultural underpinnings of their fields and the implicit values and beliefs that are specific to the dominant macroculture means that they can operate only as technicians. Second, students who belong to a minority group may lack access to what Apple and Beane (1995) referred to as "cultural capital," or the tools for success in the mainstream, and may need to be taught those rules and strategies explicitly, in a way that students who have grown up in the mainstream do not (Delpit, 1995).

In special education, personnel preparation programs explicitly teach the policies and practices of the field, explications of which can be found in any textbook or any course outlines used by teachers' colleges. As Skrtic pointed out, this process of socialization is a vital part of professional induction:

> When students can demonstrate that they have internalized the profession's knowledge, skills, norms, and values—how to think and act as professionals—they are duly certified as professionally competent by the professional school, admitted to the professional community by the relevant professional association, and licensed by the state to practice the profession. (1995b, p. 11)

However, the beliefs that underlie these policies and practices often are not made explicit and are conveyed to the initiate in forms that are so embedded as to be unacknowledged, even unrecognized, by those who teach them. Bowers (1984, 1995) referred to this knowledge as the "taken for granted" beliefs that are experienced as "the natural order of things" (Bowers, 1984, p. 36) rather than as a set of values that have been explicitly learned.

Special education is full of such embedded beliefs. An embedded belief that has received considerable attention is the way that the concept of disability becomes reified—or made into a "thing" that an individual has (Bogdan & Knoll, 1995). According to this belief, the disability is a feature of the individual's constitution and exists as objective reality. For example, Mercer (1997) argued that a learning disability reflects a factual phenomenon that exists within the brain of an individual and may be caused by a particular structural anomaly of the brain. Social constructionists, however, counter that a learning difficulty is a disability only when it is in an area of learning that is so valued by the society that its absence places the individual at a significant disadvantage. Sleeter (1986), for example, argued that after the launching of Sputnik in 1957 the growing demands of a technological economy led to a raising of reading standards, which, in turn, contributed to the establishment of the learning disability category.

The traditional approach in special education has been to assume the reification perspective. Skrtic (1991), in his analysis of the epistemological source of this perspective, pointed out that special education knowledge is grounded in the "functionalist paradigm," by which reality is viewed as objective and independent of the human perspective. He argued that in the social sciences the manifestation of functionalism that has most directly influenced the accepted special education knowledge base is functionalist psychology—in particular, psychological behaviorism and experimental psychology. Thus, in considering a spectrum of epistemological approaches from subjectivist to objectivist, Skrtic located the special education knowledge tradition "in the most extreme objectivist region of the functionalist paradigm" (1991, p. 106).

What are the implications of this view of knowledge for teacher preparation? Because, as Skrtic observed, objectivists consider this way of viewing the world as the only way, the teacher preparation process, especially in special education, typically does not require students to acknowledge other theories of knowledge. Skrtic proposed that professions are guided by a hierarchy of presuppositions, from the most abstract to the most applied, as follows: metatheories, theories, assumptions, models, practices, and tools. He argued that in special education, only the more practical rather than the theoretical levels of this hierarchy are acknowledged; that is, any criticism of special education historically has centered only on "the ethics and efficacy of its models, practices, and tools, but not on its assumptions, theories, and metatheories" (Skrtic, 1991, pp. 55–56).

Returning to the example of the reification of disabilities (the belief that disabilities are objective, pathological conditions that students have), prospective teachers may be asked to examine the efficacy of a tool, such as a psychometric test, for identifying a disability, but they are not asked to examine the underlying belief that disabilities are objective phenomena that can be objectively and accurately diagnosed by such a test (Bogdan & Knoll, 1995). By not addressing this issue, teacher preparation programs inculcate an important principle of the field at the deepest level of belief—what Bowers (1995) called the taken-for-granted level—whereby the belief represents a premise that is so embedded as to be invisible to the learner.

There are important implications of the reification perspective's going unexamined. First, this perspective reflects the medical model of disease that has been transported into the field of special education (Mercer, 1973). Society's implicit faith in the medical model leads professionals to believe that what is really a very subjective process is objective and scientific. This is particularly true for high-incidence disabilities such as learning disability, behavior disorders, and mild mental retardation. Such misplaced faith can have paradoxical results: On the one hand, the subjectivity inherent in the classification process can lead to the overrepresentation of low-performing groups in these disability categories (for a comprehensive review, see Artiles & Trent, 1994; Harry & Anderson, 1994); on the other hand, in the case of learning disability, this actually can work the other way around. In its certainty that this disability represents an intrinsic deficit, the field offers an official definition that explicitly rules out the influence of environmental factors as an explanation for the student's learning difficulties. Yet it is virtually impossible to know whether the academic difficulties of a young student, who shows no signs of developmental delay, are a result of experience or of intrinsic deficit; and the assessment instruments available do not convincingly distinguish between low-achieving students and students with a "learning disability" (Ysseldyke, Algozzine, & Thurlow, 1992). Because a student must be classified as having a disability to qualify for special education services, the exclusion of environmental effects in the classification of learning disability actually discriminates against children from low socioeconomic backgrounds or potentially detrimental social backgrounds (Collins & Camblin, 1983).

We offer the issue of reification to illustrate the tremendously complex belief systems that surround the concept of disability and to argue that such complexity demands an approach to professional preparation that will ensure a critical awareness of the entrenched beliefs that underlie special education practice. Certainly for us, this awareness has been an essential requirement of becoming members of the institution of special education as it is practiced in the United States. Being required to understand special education practices in a new society forced us to become aware of the taken-for-granted beliefs of our native institutions of education. For example, on the reification issue outlined previously, we did not differ, initially, from the traditional U.S. perspective: We also assumed that a disability was a factual phenomenon that someone has—until we noticed that people designated as having a disability in U.S. society often did not match our understanding of disabilities.

We came to see that the parameters that we used to define a disability were much broader than those being used by the U.S. school system. This was particularly true for the high-incidence disabilities such as learning disability, behavior disorders, and mild mental retardation. For example, because both of our native societies operated education systems that offered advanced education only to a minority of the population, the many children who did not show an aptitude for academic skills would not be perceived as having "disabilities"; rather, it would simply be accepted that they should pursue career goals that are not based on advanced academic skills. Thus, difficulties in learning such skills would not be perceived as outside the norm. For us, a child's difficulties would have to be quite severe before we would begin to see him or her as atypical. In fact, the notion of disability tended to be tied most often to physical anomalies or readily discernible impediments that interfered, in relatively gross ways, with interpersonal communication, social interaction, or basic academic skills.

We came to see that if we could change our view of who had a disability simply by changing the parameters of normalcy, then a disability could not be a universally recognizable, or factual, phenomenon. It became important to understand that the criteria for determining disability in the United States reflected a narrower view of normalcy than that to which we were accustomed. Two questions became important to us: How were these parameters established? What values did they represent?

As Bowers cogently stated, "The authority that culture exercises over us . . . is internalized in such a way that the person under its sway experiences it as part of the natural order of things" (1984, p. 36). The reason that we think it important for professionals to examine their taken-for-granted beliefs is that the United States is rapidly becoming the most multicultural society in the world. Although the process of acculturation is a given within such a society, it is almost always the newcomer or outsider who is required to acculturate to the ways of the mainstream, and this has been particularly detrimental to communication with families from diverse cultural backgrounds (Correa, 1989).

In special education, the result of such ethnocentric practice is that families who do not share or value the principles on which special education policies and practices are built are all too often alienated and excluded from collaboration in the treatment of their children's difficulties (Bennett, 1988; Connery, 1987; Figler, 1981; Harry, 1992a; Harry, Allen, & McLaughlin, 1995; Kalyanpur & Rao, 1991; Smith & Ryan, 1987). When families are excluded, children suffer and our attempts at remediation and support result in minimal progress for children and in frustration for professionals and families alike. The principle of family-centered practice now espoused by early interventionists points the way that is needed. Without cultural reciprocity, however, the ideal of parent–professional collaboration will continue to elude those who work with families from diverse cultures and belief systems.

The purpose of this book is to deconstruct the "natural order of things"—the value base on which the policies and practices of special education in the United States are built. The goal of such deconstruction is not to promote a laissez-faire attitude of "anything goes" as we work with people from diverse cultures but rather to advocate for a level of cultural awareness that can radically alter the ethnocentricity with which we usually approach families and communities that diverge significantly from the culture of special education. With this level of awareness, professionals can begin to develop what we describe as a "posture of cultural reciprocity."

TOWARD A POSTURE OF CULTURAL RECIPROCITY

Certain key concepts form the substance of this book. We consider these concepts to be the underpinnings on which disability policy and practice in the United States are based. In Chapter 2, we show that these concepts are both explicit and implicit in the law itself by examining the legal and epistemological underpinnings of definitions of disability. Chapter 3 illustrates how these underpinnings have an impact on the way in which professional expertise and language are conceptualized. Chapter 4 analyzes the cultural underpinnings of the "tools" of special education in professionals' recommendations to parents regarding parenting styles and goal setting for students. Finally, Chapter 5 delineates and gives examples of the "posture of cultural reciprocity," which we recommend not as a cookbook approach or a "strategy" but rather as a framework for processing what is occurring between professionals and family members. Indeed, we recommend the posture as a way of being as professionals attempt to provide services to the wide range of families that constitute the very diverse composition of U.S. society.

2

Legal and Epistemological Underpinnings of the Construction of Disability

Maya's Story

I came to the United States for the first time as a graduate student, after having taught in special schools in India for several years, and began working with adults with developmental disabilities who lived in a group home. One of the first tasks that I was assigned was to teach them "community living skills": My supervisor suggested eating in a restaurant. I set off confidently with my "client," Gary, a young man with moderate mental retardation, to the nearest restaurant; after all, I thought I knew what to expect. To me, a restaurant is a place where you go to eat; you wait to be seated; when you are seated, your waiter fetches the menu, gives you time to choose, takes your order, and soon brings your order; you eat your meal, pay the bill, leave a tip for the waiter, and leave.

Gary and I entered a McDonald's. It was the first time in my life that I had entered a fast-food restaurant, and I realized, very quickly, that the rules here were very different from what I knew. As I hesitated, Gary sized up the situation. Taking my hand, he led me to the end of a line of people who, I realized with a start, were not waiters but customers waiting to place their orders. Gary pointed to the bewildering array of choices displayed on a sign above my head—bewildering because the menu did not read from top to bottom in traditional fashion but in blocks across the wall. I looked at the first block and began to make a choice when, as I came to the end of the list, I discovered that this block was for breakfast only and not available after 10 A.M. Then I looked at the second block and started to choose from the list when Gary directed my attention to the third block; I learned later that the second block was for specialty items. It seemed that despite the array of choices, our impecunious circumstances restricted us to a single option: the value meals in the third block.

By the time I had recognized the subtle differences between a "number one value meal" (cheeseburger, fries, and a medium drink) and a "number two value meal" (double cheeseburger, fries, and a medium drink), we had reached the front of the line. But before I could say anything, the lady behind the counter said, "For-here-to-go?" I stared absolutely blankly at her. What on earth did that mean? Was she speaking in English? When I did not respond immediately, Gary stepped up and replied, "Here." With obvious relief, the woman turned to him and directed all subsequent questions, including my order, to him. We carried our trays to a small table to which Gary led us; later, he showed me how to "bus" our table.

In that environment, I undoubtedly was the more disabled of the two, not only in my own perception but also in others'. Over the years, I have related this story to my students on numerous occasions as a springboard for a discussion on the social construction of disability. It serves to remind me of the fragility of our own perceptions of competence and helps them to become aware of the arbitrariness with which we determine, in each culture, who is "normal."

The arguments in this chapter are based on the premise that the parameters for normalcy or deviance are socially constructed. The view that disability is a matter of perspective is not new. Several social theorists have argued that disability is constructed relative to particular social and cultural practices and independent of the loss of a bodily function, cognitive or physical (Barton, 1996; Bérubé, 1996; Bogdan & Knoll, 1995; Fulcher, 1989, 1996; Goode, 1992; McDermott & Varenne, 1995). Indeed, the question of what is a disabling condition and who is disabled (the meaning of disability), and who makes these decisions (the models that establish these meanings) is specific to a culture. Although in some cultures the meaning of disability is established by legal or professional institutions, in other cultures these meanings may emerge more from "folk beliefs" (Groce & Zola, 1993) and from community understanding of people's roles (Edwards, 1997; Helander, 1995). In turn, societal values influence both models and meanings.

Research on attitudes toward people with disabilities in different cultures (e.g., Danseco, 1997b) points to differences in the meaning of disability. Findings indicate that the same condition may or may not be perceived as a disability in different societies and that certain conditions may carry more of a stigma than others. For instance, some Yoruba families perceive physical conditions such as goiter, hunchback, and albinism to be punishments for offenses against God and therefore a disgrace; conversely, hydrocephalus is neither a stigma nor a disability (Walker, 1986). Some Asian families consider having a child with a developmental disability a sign of good fortune in the future, others view it as a punishment of past sins, and many consider it an act of God that cannot be changed (Miles, 1997).

Findings also reveal that the value attached to a certain disabling condition differs depending on societal expectations and the established parameters for normalcy. For example, among the Manus of New Guinea, because being able to handle a canoe is a necessary survival skill, the loss of an arm is much more of a disability and much more stigmatizing than the inability to read (Edgerton, 1970). Conversely, technological availability of prosthetic devices and societal expectations for literacy in the United States combine to create exactly opposite perceptions of the same disabilities.

An analysis of education and rehabilitation policies also indicates differing interpretations of disability (Barton, 1996; Fulcher, 1989; Mehan, 1988; Skrtic, 1995b). For instance, in many capitalist economies, nonproductive people—that is, those who do not contribute to the growth of the economy—are perceived as dependent or disabled (Hahn, 1986; Margonis, 1992). As Fulcher pointed out,

> Disability is a *disputed* category. This is clear when we look at welfare state and education practices. Its relevance is disputed: Is this, or isn't it, a case of disability? And if so, how much, how disabled? Is this person feigning incapacity? Is this doctor working to lower the company's liability? Or is he/she, the doctor, making an unbiased judgment? The way social institutions should respond (segregate or integrate?) and how (with what resources?): These are all contentious issues. Disability is thus *struggled over* in social practices in a range of arenas; it is a *procedural and political category.* (1989, p. 24; italics in original)

Similarly, education policy requires that students be evaluated to determine their eligibility for special education services, a process that results in labeling some students by disability category. As a result, 10.4% of all children between the ages of 6 and 17 are identified as having special education needs and receive some services (McDonnell, McLaughlin, & Morison, 1997). When we examine who acquires or who is more likely to acquire the identity of being disabled, however, we discover an overrepresentation of 1) poor (McDonnell et al., 1997), 2) culturally and linguistically diverse (Heller, Holtzman, & Messick, 1982; McDonnell et al., 1997; Mercer, 1973), and 3) male (Athans, 1998; Turnbull & Turnbull, 1998) students in special education. It would appear that the assessment process results in the labeling of many students as having a disability, even though they may not have an impairment.

The two sections of this chapter examine the implications of the cultural specificity of the models and meanings of disability for families whose points of view may differ. The first section consists of two parts. First, it identifies some of the values that underlie special education law and policy in the United States, specifically the Individuals with Disabilities Education Act (IDEA) of 1990 (PL 101-476) and its amendments of 1997 (PL 105-17). Next, it discusses the implications of this value embeddedness for families from contrasting traditions. The second section also has two parts. First, it identifies certain assumptions about the meaning of disability contained within the dominant epistemological paradigm, the medical model, within the context of the overrepresentation in special education of students from culturally and linguistically diverse backgrounds. Next, it shows how these meanings may contrast with the beliefs of minority families.

CULTURAL UNDERPINNINGS OF SPECIAL EDUCATION LAW

Education and social policies reflect the core values of prevailing cultural contexts (Marshall, Mitchell, & Wirt, 1989; Welles-Nyström, 1996). Indeed, as Marshall et al. noted, "We can learn a great deal about a culture by understanding [its] values . . . and by understanding the ways in which values are built into policy" (1989, p. 6). For instance, in a study of Swedish family policy, Welles-Nyström (1996) identified the ideology of equality as the underpinning for Swedish child health care policies. That is, the rights of women to participate in the labor force and of men to participate in the home and in child care are ensured through legislation for both maternity and paternity leave, and children's rights are ensured through numerous legislative measures, including the socialized health care sector for all children, regardless of race or socioeconomic status.

That social policy is a response to the cultural context becomes clear when we examine policy changes in the United States over time. For instance, during the latter half of the 19th century, the ideal of individualism as a striving for self-reliance and independence was tied to the national civic goal of efficient and rapid economic development (Marshall et al., 1989). Thus, social policy reflected efficiency measures that sought to exclude those who did not conform to this mold. Concerns about "new" immigrants from southwestern Europe who might not subscribe to American values (Valdés, 1996) and attempts to classify races led to federal immigration laws that severely limited immigration (Tyack, 1993). Dependent individuals—for instance, people with developmental disabilities—also were perceived to be undesirable, and their reproductive capability was restricted through compulsory sterilization acts and large-scale warehousing in institutions (Rauscher & McClintock, 1997).

It is only in the latter half of the 20th century that the ideal of equity has emerged as the preeminent value and has broadened to encompass disenfranchised groups, including women, people of color, people with disabilities, and children—the primary beneficiaries of social and education policy—and allowed them the freedom to make their own life choices (Friedman, 1996; Marshall et al., 1989). Simultaneously, the concept of individualism began to embrace freedom of choice, individual rights, and autonomy as its defining factors (Friedman, 1990). As a result, attitudes toward people with disabilities changed dramatically, influencing through public policy and legal reform an equally profound change in people's quality of life from rejection and segregation to acceptance and inclusion (Ferguson, 1994; Jablow, 1992; Turnbull & Turnbull, 1998). The emergence of new ideologies in human services, such as the principle of normalization, which involves making the lives of people with disabilities as normal as is practicable (Wolfensberger, 1972), and the principle of the least restrictive environment (LRE), which provides an array of programmatic options for students with disabilities to maximize their potential (Turnbull & Turnbull, 1998), further reinforced this emphasis on equity, choice, and individual rights.

We contend that this interaction of attitude and political beliefs with legal doctrine that resulted in compatible ideologies in human services and special education programs occurs within a cultural context. For instance, the movement toward deinstitutionalization on the basis of the principle of normalization emerged from the societal emphasis on rights and individualism (Biklen, 1974; Wolfensberger, 1972). Similarly, the self-advocacy and parents' movements used the platform of rights and equality to further their causes; both ideals eventually became the cornerstone principles for special education legislation, such as IDEA (Mallory, 1995; Miller & Keys, 1996; Turnbull & Turnbull, 1997). Indeed, IDEA is a product of 20th-century American culture. As Marshall et al. pointed out, "Laws are ultimately statements about particular values that dominate within a political system. Such values reflect cultures" (1989, p. 138).

IDEA as a Cultural Statement

IDEA encompasses six principles of law:

1. *Zero reject,* or the right of every child to education
2. *Nondiscriminatory assessment,* or the right to a fair evaluation to determine appropriate educational placement
3. *Individualized and appropriate education* to ensure that the education is meaningful
4. *Least restrictive environment* to ensure that children with disabilities can associate with typical peers to the maximum extent appropriate to their needs
5. *Due process* to ensure the child's right to challenge any aspect of education
6. *Parent participation,* which allows parents to participate in the education decision-making process (for a fuller description, see Turnbull & Turnbull, 1998)

An analysis of these six principles reveals several core underlying values. Although we acknowledge that other values may be represented in these principles, for the purpose of our analysis, we focus on three core values: individualism, equity, and choice. We also recognize that each principle may have many more underlying values than those presented here; however, to illustrate our argument, we identify the most overt representations. (Indeed, so subtly are the values embedded that few recognize that the term *least restrictive environment,* which forms the philosophical basis for special education program options, originates from the capitalist concept of free trade.) For instance, the value of individualism underlies the principles of due process and individualized, appropriate education, whereas the principles of parent participation and the LRE are grounded in the right to freedom of choice. Similarly, the value of equity is embedded in the principles of zero reject, nondiscriminatory assessment, and parent participation.

We also discuss the implications of these value-embedded principles for families of children with disabilities who may not subscribe to the same values and must negotiate what Cutler (1993) referred to as the "special education maze." It is not our purpose to impute invidious intent to IDEA because it is a product of mainstream culture; as such, it is most aptly suited to the values and, therefore, the needs of the members of the culture (although some might argue that its implementation has rendered it less effective). Nevertheless, this implicit congruence of value system and policy may be problematic for culturally diverse families.

Individualism in IDEA   The principle of individualized and appropriate education operationalizes the idea that all children have the right to education and that this education must be meaningful and appropriate to each individual's level of skills. Based on the assumption that the individual, not society, comes first, the focus for all education service programming is on the individual; for instance, "person-centered planning" (Turnbull & Turnbull, 1997) places the individual with disabilities at the center of a universe that consists of pertinent domains, such as home, school, and community. Although in an individualized family service plan (IFSP) the unit of analysis might shift a little to accommodate the family, the focus is still on the infant or the toddler with disabilities as professionals identify supports and services that families may need to meet the child's needs.

Furthermore, because the purpose of education is to provide students with the skills that they would need to acquire a job and become independent, productive adults (Margonis, 1992), the underlying assumption in this principle is that a meaningful education for children with disabilities maximizes their potential toward the ultimate goal of independence: open, competitive employment (Powers, Singer, & Sowers, 1996). Such a high value is placed on individuals' becoming self-reliant and responsible for making their own life choices that these outcomes are a major part of most individualized education programs (IEPs). Thus, the concept of individualism is embedded in the notions of maximization of potential, competitive open employment, and self-reliance and autonomy.

In the principle of procedural due process, individualism provides the underpinning for the idea that all citizens have rights that are protected under the law; indeed, parents of children with disabilities have the right to be told their rights specific to their child's education. Similarly, a major aspect of self-advocacy curriculum consists of informing people with disabilities of their rights so that they can demand their entitlements and protest if denied them. Implicit in this argument is the individualistic belief that people are responsible for ensuring their own protection. In other words, although the statutes entitle individuals to protection under the law, ensuring that protection is up to the person, as this action guide for parents illustrates:

> If you buy a toaster that doesn't work as it's supposed to, you take action. . . . You don't wring your hands and wait for the company to find you. It's the same with IDEA. . . . The full implementation of the law depends on parents. (Cutler, 1993, p. 3)

An important aspect of this notion of personal responsibility and self-determination is the right to protest, possibly the most individualistic feature of the principle of due process. Litigation is a process of dispute resolution that involves formal legal mechanisms; the process can be initiated by ordinary citizens and is not imposed from the top down (Turnbull & Turnbull, 1998). Friedman (1996) argued that the tendency to sue is a structural and cultural feature of American society that emerges from modern individualism. As he stated, "It would be hard to imagine much litigation among people who truly believe that it is wrong to make a fuss, or who value harmony and compromise above most other values" (Friedman, 1996, p. 58). What is most significant is that it assumes that individuals would be able to assume the level of assertiveness that is needed for claiming their rights and be aware of the appropriate avenues for redress, as this example of an African American mother illustrates. On discovering that her daughter with disabilities was to be placed in a program that was inappropriate to her needs, A. Johnson did the following:

> I called the local television stations and told them that I'd been trying to communicate with the [school] district and they wouldn't [respond], and somebody sent a camera team out to the district office and I had a little picket sign that said the school district would not talk to parents, only media. And I walked up and down with that sign for awhile and no one from the school district came out. So finally I just went into the office of one of the school district's personnel and talked to them. And after having tried to resolve that problem for maybe a week or so, it was resolved that afternoon. (Personal communication, April 29, 1997)

Friedman suggested that the increase in litigation is in part due to the increase in the scope of the law to a point that almost all areas of life are "potentially justiciable" (1990, p. 16). By mandating an education for all children with disabilities, for instance, the legal system opened the door for parents to protest the violation of this right. The paradox is that although the mandate for parent participation requires school personnel to involve parents in the decision-making process and establish collaborative partnerships, the principle of due process pits parents and professionals against each other and creates adversarial conditions.

Choice in IDEA   Implicit in the right to freedom of choice are the individualistic beliefs that each person may—indeed, has the right to—aspire to the valued goal of upward social mobility (although the reality of achievement is not guaranteed) and that no individual should be placed at a disadvantage as a result of "immutable characteristics," or those aspects of self that are not within a person's choice, such as disability or gender (Friedman, 1996). In other words, all citizens have the right to the pursuit of happiness and can choose how they wish to attain this goal. Society then distinguishes those who appear to be capable and choose not to, for instance, in the commonly held perception that the poor are lazy and poor of their own making, and those who cannot because they possess an immutable characteristic.

Certain legal provisions guarantee freedom of choice to ensure that individuals are not placed at a disadvantage because they cannot choose their personal characteristics. Although these compensatory provisions—top-down measures—could be interpreted as welfare or charity, they are defined as entitlements, or rights, that support an independent way of life (Friedman, 1990). In other words, the opportunities to make choices are "rights, not favors" (Cutler, 1993, p. 9), precisely because they enable autonomy and choice making. This distinction of "rights, not favors" is crucial because it contributes to the culture of individual ownership that enhances the sense of personal outrage and, as noted previously, raises the likelihood of conflict resolution through confrontation rather than mediation or "simply swallowing one's anger" (Friedman, 1996, p. 58).

In IDEA, choice is embedded in the principles of LRE and parent participation. The principle of LRE, through its programmatic model of a cascade of services (Turnbull, Turnbull, Shank, & Leal, 1999), is most closely identified with the value of choice. In its original intention, this model of services ran along a continuum of environments from most segregated and with the highest intensity of services to least segregated and with the lowest intensity of services (Taylor, 1988) to provide the most individualized—almost customized—educational, vocational, and residential environments for students and adults with disabilities (Bruininks & Lakin, 1985). Similarly, the principle of parent participation, in giving parents the right, among others, to choose from this range of programmatic options, exemplifies the "socialized expectation of participatory democracy" (Marshall et al., 1989, p. 70) that citizens have some choice in decisions about services that they use (Marshall et al., 1989; Peterson & Noyes, 1997; Ravitch, 1997). Furthermore, challenging the emphasis on professional decision making, the principle that parents should participate in school policy and programming is another assertion of the choice value.

We acknowledge that, in reality, however, most parents do not have much choice, in terms of services. Policy analysts suggest that this is because there is an inherent tension between equity and choice: Equity increases as choice decreases (Margonis, 1992; Marshall et al., 1989; Ravitch, 1997). The tension exists in terms of how resources are allocated. The greater the effort made to distribute resources and services equitably, the less the choice for the recipients of these services. When given more choice for interpretation, school systems often will decide that providing individualized, choice-based services for all is not feasible and that distributing equitably without personal choice is better than offering choices to some and leaving few or no resources for many (Marshall et al., 1989).

Equity in IDEA   The value of equity is embedded in the principles of zero reject, nondiscriminatory assessment, and parent participation. Behind the principle of zero reject is a long history that overlays the value of equity. As the role of a child came to be perceived increasingly as that of student, schooling for all children was mandated to avoid inequities and was made available through universal primary education (Turnbull & Turnbull, 1998). Next, arguments against racial segregation in schools were made on the grounds of inequity, that separate schools provided inferior education to certain groups of students on the basis of an immutable characteristic—their race—and placed them at a disadvantage for making equal life choices (Ravitch, 1997). These precedents provided the framework for mandating an education for students with disabilities; excluding students with disabilities from public schools was a discriminatory act because the basis for exclusion was their disability, another immutable characteristic. In addition, the equal protection and equal access doctrines provided the context for the zero-reject policy. Now, students with disabilities cannot be denied an education; furthermore, the education that they receive must enable them as adults to have access to the same life choices as people without disabilities.

Equity also is the underpinning of the principle of nondiscriminatory evaluation. For instance, the mandate for fair assessment and labeling is based on the recognition that classifying students as having a disability when they do not or classifying them incorrectly may deny them equal opportunities to an education (Turnbull & Turnbull, 1998). Furthermore, it acknowledges that there is a disproportionate representation of culturally and linguistically diverse students in special education, which would indicate discrimination on the grounds of race and cultural background (Heller et al., 1982; IDEA Amendments of 1997).

Finally, the ideal of participatory democracy is embedded in the principle of parent participation, which entitles parents to share as equal partners with professionals in the decision-making process of their child's education. On the understanding that parents act on behalf of their minor child, this principle ensures parents' rights to exercise their child's rights to an education. As noted previously, however, when placed in conjunction with the principle of due process, this requirement creates adversarial conditions between parents and professionals. Furthermore, school districts all too often prefer to abide by the letter, not the spirit, of the law so that parent participation is more "compliance than communication" (Harry, Allen, & McLaughlin, 1995). Because policy determines special education practice, it is crucial that professionals become aware of these cultural underpinnings, particularly when dealing with families who may not uphold these values and may have differing concepts of self, immutable characteristics, and status.

Contrasting Cultural Traditions

One of the aims of contemporary mainstream American society is to foster individual growth and maximize choices that are open to all individuals equally. This ideal is embodied in the principles of special education law in an effort to ensure that students with disabilities, like all others, have equal opportunities for education in order to maximize life choices and to develop independence and self-reliance and that parents, too, may participate in a democratic decision-making process toward ensuring this outcome. These constructs assume that both the underlying values and the outcomes are highly regarded universally. This section discusses the implications for families who, in fact, subscribe neither to these values nor to the social outcomes.

Alternative Concepts of Self Various aspects of the value of individualism, such as the notion that the individual (not society) comes first, freedom of choice, and rights consciousness (including the right to protest and the right to maximize one's potential), are embedded in the principles of individualized and appropriate education and procedural due process. These concepts of individualism, however, may be antithetical to the beliefs of many families with children with disabilities, which may lead to some dissonance when planning an individualized and appropriate education. For example, some families—for instance, Asians—traditionally may subscribe to a concept of self whereby individual identity cannot be separated from the group—that, indeed, it is a product of the group (Brady & Anderson, 1983; Ross-Sheriff, 1992; Wong, 1989). Because individual needs are subservient to those of the community, a "culture of duties" (Chung, 1992b, p. 128) prevails where individuals have ascribed social responsibilities (Schweder, Mahapatra, & Miller, 1990). For instance, Wong noted that the values of participatory democracy and individual rights conflict with traditional Chinese values of propriety and individual duties:

> The Chinese conception of the individual, in contrast to the Kantian tradition, is not one of an abstract entity. Here, roles and statuses determine one's dignity; difference in abilities are believed to be relevant in evaluating one's worth; one's behaviors are very much constrained by social identity and the related obligations it imposes. As such, it is not difficult to understand why the Western conceptions of "rights" and "equality" are so foreign to the Chinese. (1989, p. 97)

In such a context, families may be both unfamiliar and uncomfortable with the prevailing "culture of rights" on which American special education policy and, therefore, practice are based (Bean & Thorburn, 1995; Holdsworth, 1995). Studies indicate that families that have recently immigrated from countries where schooling was not the norm for children are most likely to be unaware of their child's right to education, particularly in cases in which the child has a disability, or of their right to protest if their child's rights are violated (Dentler & Hafner, 1997; Valdés, 1996). Furthermore, even after having been made aware of their rights, they may be unable to assume the level of assertiveness needed for claiming them. For instance, the organizer of a support group of Vietnamese families of children with disabilities described a problem that he faced in helping the families gain access to services: "People are afraid of asking for favors. . . . I try to show them, to explain to them that they have the right to ask for the services and they are not asking for a favor" (N. Chu, personal communication, April 9, 1997).

Similarly, other scholars have noted that the individualism that is embedded in family–school policies places the onus on parents for initiating involvement in their child's education (Hadaway & Marek-Schroer, 1992; Lareau & Shumar, 1996), an expectation that can be unfair to parents who are "hampered by modesty, language differences, mistrust, and defensive attitudes or who may not have the necessary background and knowledge about assessment procedures and special programs in the schools" (Hadaway & Marek-Schroer, 1992, p. 76). Some newly immigrated parents have misunderstood the professional recommendation to place their child in "special" education for remedial programming to mean that their child has an extraordinary talent that merits placement in a gifted program (Cloud, 1993).

In some families, parents might perceive that their children have little authority to make their own decisions; should there be a discrepancy between what the parents want for their children and what the children want for themselves, the parents' expectations prevail. In such situations, parents are unlikely to believe that their children have rights and even less likely to recognize any violations of these rights. This perspective might lead to conflict when professionals, who come from a more individualistic belief system, want to overrule the parents' wishes in favor of the child's desires. Such situations are particularly acute when the child involved is a young adult and the parents' conception of the age of majority does not match policy and legislation (Mallory, 1992). For instance, in *Wisconsin v. Yoder* (1972), although the Mennonite parents decided that their high school graduate son had had enough schooling and forbade him to pursue further education, a court of law ruled that the young adult, having attained majority, had the right to continue his education, if he so chose, and that his rights to education were being violated.

Differing Perceptions of Immutable Characteristics

Choice is such a highly regarded American value that equity-based legislation seeks to ensure that individuals who possess a trait—an "immutable characteristic"—that could reduce their chances for making choices toward the pursuit of happiness will not be denied these opportunities. Other groups, however, may not regard individual choice as highly and may severely proscribe personal choices on many aspects (Chung, 1992a; Mohan, 1992). For instance, some societies do not allow individuals a choice in the matter of religion (Ross-Sheriff, 1992); some families restrict their adolescent children in the choices that they make about making friends, choosing an occupation, and selecting a life partner (Mohan, 1992). By the same token, a trait, such as gender, that in one culture may be perceived as an immutable characteristic justifying equity-based legislation may in another culture be interpreted as justifying specific acts of discrimination. For instance, among some Indian (Mohan, 1992), Muslim (Ross-Sheriff & Nanji, 1991, cited in

Ross-Sheriff, 1992), and Chinese (Chung, 1992a) families, the belief
that a woman need not work outside the home or have a career often precluded girls from receiving an education or pursuing any
academic goals more ambitious than an elementary education.

Parents for whom choice is not a highly regarded value may
not expect to be presented with an array of special education service options (Smith & Ryan, 1987); should a school district choose
not to inform parents about the various programs and services that
are available, the families may not even be aware that their right to
freedom of choice is being violated. Indeed, the onus is on parents
to identify the types of available options and become informed
about the appropriateness of these various programs for their child
with disabilities. This presumes a high level of awareness and re-
sourcefulness in parents that may be unfair (Lareau & Shumar,
1996). For instance, in Harry's (1998) study of culturally diverse
families, the parents readily agreed to have their children with disabilities participate in inclusive programs when informed of these
options by the researchers; despite the inclusive nature of the
child's family environments, none of the families had questioned
the school system's decision to place their child in segregated environments, primarily because they had not known that they had a
choice.

Principle of Value Inequality In the United States, the
ideal of equality is so much a part of our collective conscience that
we often are unaware of this underlying value in our professional
policy. This emphasis on equality, however, may be antithetical to
many families who may believe instead in the fundamental tenet of
"the value-inequality of human beings, by reason of birth, caste,
skin pigmentation, economic, and social status" (Miles, 1981, p. 7).
For instance, Wong (1989) noted that among some Chinese families, people are assumed to have different capacities and status ow-
ing to different backgrounds (e.g., education) and characteristics
(e.g., age); it is therefore accepted that some people should dominate others because of their status. Similarly, because social roles
and duties are ascribed among many Indian (Mohan, 1992) and Korean (Song-Kim, 1992) families, the status of various family members is predetermined in terms of a hierarchical order: Elders have
high status, men have higher status than women, and children assert their authority according to birth order. Indeed, Schweder et
al. noted that to many Hindu families, "the justice of received differences and inequalities, . . . (the) asymmetrical interdependen-
cies in nature (for example, parent–child), and the vulnerabilities

and differential rationalities of social actors [are] universal truths" (1990, p. 160).

To prevent the abuse of power in hierarchical structures, there is the expectation that those in more privileged positions will recognize their obligations toward the less privileged, a sort of "noblesse oblige," also known as "li," or rules of propriety, in China (Chung, 1992b; Wong, 1989), or "dharma" in India (Fishlock, 1983; Kalyanpur, 1996). By the same standard, professionals, by virtue of their higher status, have a similar duty toward protecting and ensuring their clients' well-being. This understanding conflicts dramatically with the idea of individual responsibility, which places the onus for advocacy on parents.

Thus the belief in value inequality has tremendous implications for parents whose children are in the special education system, particularly with regard to the policy expectation for parent participation. The perception that a professional is a person of high standing and a figure of authority makes it difficult for parents to participate as equal partners in education decision making (Harry, 1992a, 1992c, 1992e; Smith & Ryan, 1987). Many parents do not participate because they have had a history of bad experiences with schooling and do not perceive that the power dynamics between them and the professionals has changed; this is particularly true of many low-income (Lareau & Shumar, 1996) and African American (Harry, 1992e; Harry, Allen, & McLaughlin, 1996) families. Other parents may attend IEP meetings, but their silence at these occasions may be due to deference to authority and compliance, even disagreement (Harry, 1992c, 1992e; Harry, Allen, & McLaughlin, 1995).

Some families may also become uncomfortable with the professional expectation that their child with disabilities be "normalized" (Wolfensberger, 1972)—that is, given the opportunities to lead a normal rhythm of life with outcome and quality of life consonant with that of the child's peers. This effort to level the playing field for children with disabilities is based on an ideal of equality for all children, including all siblings in a family. As indicated by Harry's (1998) study of culturally diverse families, however, although parents might aspire to give their child with disabilities the best life possible, even referring to it as "a normal life," they do not mean a life that is the same as for the other siblings, arguing that perforce the outcomes for the child with disabilities will be different, just as the outcomes for the oldest or the male child will be different from that of the younger or the female children.

CULTURAL UNDERPINNINGS OF
SPECIAL EDUCATION EPISTEMOLOGY

The previous section analyzed the cultural underpinnings of special education law to illustrate how the cultural specificity of these values can become a source of conflict for families who may have diverse, even opposing, points of view and value systems. As we have stated before, our intention is not to imply that the law is inappropriate—indeed, quite the opposite, for a law that upholds and protects the most highly cherished values of the majority of the people is perfectly suited to its purpose—but to indicate that, for some, albeit a minority, these values may not be consonant with their worldview, thus contributing to the possibility of parent–professional dissonance.

This section examines the cultural specificity of the meaning of disability embedded in special education professional knowledge. In low-context cultures such as the United States (Hall, 1981), where "social relationships and contexts are more impersonal and task specific, and individuals are not related to each other in varied contexts" (Scheer & Groce, 1988, p. 31), a single immutable characteristic, such as disability, may be used to classify and denote the individual's social identity. This process is formalized through institutions (or models) that include laws, administrative procedures, medical diagnoses, welfare institutions, professional specializations, and business interests (Whyte & Ingstad, 1995). These institutions are a part of the local social and civic consciousness and can—and do—influence members' attitudes and values (Hall, 1981). Their greater legitimacy and authority are due to the positivistic belief that the knowledge that they provide is tantamount to the "truth" because it is assumed to be scientific and, therefore, objective (Hall, 1981; Skrtic, 1995a). As Whyte and Ingstad noted,

> Western conceptions of disability are formed in the context of a centralist state that imposes a universal code through legislation. Stiker (1982) argued that legislation gives to infirmity an existence and a consistency it never had before—definition, criteria, and degrees of severity. (1995, p. 8)

Special education professional knowledge owes its epistemological origins to the similarly positivist fields of medicine, psychiatry, and psychology, in particular, experimental psychology, which provides the basis for education's psychometric approach to assessment and evaluation (Skrtic, 1995a). The roots of these fields are, in turn, embedded in Western rationalist thought. Thus, the definition of disability as "a biological or physical impairment" (Nicolaisen, 1995, p. 39) emerges from this cultural framework.

Clinical Perspective

The paradigm that has dominated professional knowledge in special education is the clinical perspective, or the medical model (Mercer, 1973). This perspective of deviance contains two contrasting theories of normalcy: the pathological model from medicine and the statistical model from psychology. The pathological model defines abnormality according to the presence of observable biological symptoms, whereas the absence of these symptoms connotes good health, and it implies that abnormality is an unhealthy state that requires alleviation or "fixing." The statistical model, which is based on the concept of the normal curve, defines abnormality according to the extent to which an individual varies from the average of a population on a particular attribute, and it implies an inherent evaluative neutrality in that it is society that defines whether deviance from the average on a certain attribute is good or bad. Whereas instances of moderate to severe developmental disabilities that have distinct etiologies and characteristics come under the rubric of the pathological model, conditions that are considered mild and that do not have specific biological characteristics come under the rubric of the statistical model, as in a low score on an IQ test. Because a low IQ score is stigmatizing socially, however, mental retardation is regarded as a pathological condition, an objective attribute of the individual (Mercer, 1973; Skrtic, 1995a).

The dominance of this clinical perspective in the field of special education has led to two consequences that are of concern to us. First, its legal and professional procedures combine to construct an identity of *disabled* that often is unrelated to the actual idea of cognitive or physical bodily functioning. This is indicated by the fact, noted previously, that some groups, such as poor, culturally and linguistically diverse, and male students, tend to be identified and placed in special education programs more than others. Second, it overlooks the fact that the meaning of disability is not universal and that some families' perceptions about what is a disability and who is disabled may differ from that of the clinical perspective.

Deconstructing the clinical perspective of disability yields four implicit assumptions:

1. Disability is a physical phenomenon.
2. Disability is an individual phenomenon.
3. Disability is a chronic illness.

4. Disability requires remediation or "fixing" (Bogdan & Knoll; 1995; Mercer, 1973; Skrtic, 1995a, 1995b).

This section examines each of these assumptions, the first two with particular regard to the issue of overrepresentation of linguistically and culturally diverse students. This is followed by an analysis of the social systems perspective that offers contrasting meanings of disability.

Disability Is a Physical Phenomenon The Western rationalist belief system and, therefore, the field of medicine dichotomize the spirit and the body, imputing physical causes to all disabling conditions (Fadiman, 1997), including those that affect the mind, such as mental illness, which is attributed to neurochemical imbalances in the brain. Accordingly, a disability is assumed to have a biological etiology and an identifiable set of symptoms that constitute that disability; in turn, any individual who exhibits a minimum number of symptoms that are characteristic of a particular syndrome is assumed to have that specific disability.

Similarly, given the logic that all disabling conditions must have a physical or biological cause, professionals in the special education system determine certain student characteristics to be symptomatic of a specific category of disability; the legal definition of the category reifies this determination. Next, professionals identify which students exhibit these characteristics through both informal means, such as classroom observations, and formal means, such as standardized assessment tests. Furthermore, because current policy requires that a student be deemed either to have or not to have a disability for educational purposes, established eligibility criteria are used to ascertain the presence of a disability.

This process is based on two taken-for-granted beliefs. First, it assumes that the problem is intrinsic to the child and that there are no contextual explanations, such as environment or culture, for the behavior (Harry & Anderson, 1994; Mercer, 1973; Skrtic, 1995a). For instance, the official definition of *learning disability* explicitly excludes environmental, cultural, and economic effects as possible causes (IDEA Amendments of 1997). Second, it assumes that identification occurs through a scientific and objective process because professionals are involved. These assumptions have significant implications for students from culturally, linguistically, and socioeconomically diverse backgrounds.

One problem is that approximately 90% of the children who are classified as having disabilities in school environments are accounted for by just 4 of the 13 categories, often referred to as the "judgment" categories—learning disabilities, speech and language impairments, mental retardation, and severe emotional disturbance—for which there are no clearly identifiable biological bases; learning disabilities account for more than 50% of all classified students, and the impairments in behavior are restricted to specific roles in specific contexts (McDonnell, McLaughlin, & Morison, 1997). In other words, almost 90% of students in special education have difficulties in specific contexts only. Because the medical model does not allow for nonphysical or contextual explanations for a behavior, however, a student's specific difficulty is interpreted as an impairment that is inherent in the student and that occurs across all contexts.

Second, many students are placed in special education programs by a process that in reality involves a high level of professional subjectivity. For instance, teacher referral is the leading reason that students are screened for service eligibility despite vast variations in teacher tolerance for student behaviors (Algozzine, 1977; Hadaway & Marek-Schroer, 1992; Mehan, 1988). The idiosyncratic nature of the labeling process is powerfully illustrated by a study by Mehan (1988), which found that although teachers would allow behavior (e.g., hitting a classmate) from some students, they would not permit this inappropriate social behavior from other students whom they had already targeted and identified for intervention.

Some writers have suggested that many professionals might misinterpret the behavioral and verbal style of their minority students, frequently resulting in inappropriate classification (Delpit, 1995; Harry, 1994; Harry & Anderson, 1994; Kalyanpur, 1995). For instance, Delpit (1995) noted that, often, African American students, coming from home environments where they are more familiar with the imperative, "Put the scissors in the box," are misperceived as being defiant when they do not comply immediately with their Anglo American teachers' less directive instruction, "The scissors go in the box." Harry and Anderson (1994) asserted that the disproportionate numbers of African American males from low socioeconomic backgrounds who are placed in programs for students with severe emotional disturbance (SED) particularly indicates the cultural relativity of student behavior and teacher judgment.

The arbitrariness of classification processes is also indicated by changes that have occurred in eligibility criteria. For instance, by reducing from 85 to 70 the IQ cutoff point for mild mental retardation in the official definition, the meaning of *mental retardation* was changed overnight (Hardman, Drew, & Egan, 1999). Wide variations

among states in classification policies, including differences in terminology, key dimensions, and classification criteria, are another
indication:

> It is highly unlikely that there are over nine times as many students
> with mental retardation in Alabama as in New Jersey; that there are
> over three times as many students with SLD [specific learning disabili-
> ties] in Massachusetts as in Georgia; or that there are 40 times as many
> students with SED in Connecticut as in Mississippi. . . . These varia-
> tions are more likely to be related to unique state-by-state practices
> regarding how children and youth are identified as disabled than to
> real differences in student populations. (McDonnell, McLaughlin, &
> Morison, 1997, p. 76)

At stake is the issue of who gets labeled. Although the potential
for misclassification exists for a majority of students, the explicit
exclusion of environmental factors places poor and culturally and
linguistically diverse students at greater risk. If we recognize that a
disability, particularly the high-incidence categories that lack
clearly defined etiologies, is in reality a set of criteria that are established by professionals and that are subject to change and are very
vulnerable to individual interpretation, then we become aware of
the possibility that many students may be wrongly labeled and
placed in special education programs. Thus, we realize that there is
little, if any, justification for the overrepresentation of students from
culturally and linguistically diverse backgrounds in special education programs, particularly in the four judgment categories (Harry,
1992d, 1994; Harry & Anderson, 1994; McDonnell et al., 1997; Mercer, 1973).

Disability Is an Individual Phenomenon   A second
implication of the medicalized view is the extent to which ownership of learning or developmental disabilities is seen as belonging
to the individual or to the group. A medicalized attribution of disability locates the problem within the individual rather than within
the family, unless there is clear evidence of genetic etiology. Monks
and Frankenberg suggested that this focus emerges from the notion
of personhood in Western industrialized societies wherein "the location of individuality in consciousness has been associated with
an emphasis on rationality, responsibility, and the continuity of a
self that exists independently of both the sociocultural environment
and bodily changes" (1995, p. 107).

This point of view has two paradoxical assumptions. On the
one hand, in mainstream American culture, a medicalized explanation of disability generally is seen as mitigating stigma because the

condition is viewed as an accident of nature, an event beyond our control for which nobody can be blamed (with the exception of conditions with a clear biological etiology, such as fetal alcohol syndrome). The increasing reliance on this kind of belief is evident in the medicalizing of substance abuse or, in the field of education, hyperactivity (Conrad, 1976). Even when a condition is thought to be genetically determined, the notion of blame is not part of the diagnosis.

On the other hand, a medicalized explanation attributes a child's failure in school to a difference within him or her in a context in which, as Artiles (1998) argued, difference is linked to abnormality or stigma and, by the same token, sameness is synonymous with equality. Referring to this phenomenon as the "dilemma of difference," he noted that, difference being a comparative term, mainstream American culture represents the norm against which comparisons are made; as a result, minority people traditionally have been defined for what they are not, for example, non-Caucasian, and "deficit thinking has permeated dominant conceptions of minority people" (Artiles, 1998, p. 4). When all students are compared with the norm of the majority Caucasian culture, students who might have different cognitive and verbal skills that represent "concepts formed through exposure, experience, and their unique backgrounds" (Roseberry-McKibbin, 1995, p. 14) are perceived to have a deficit (Artiles, 1998; Roseberry-McKibbin, 1995).

Much has been written on the fundamental flaws in standardized tests and diagnostic tools used for measuring IQ, particularly for students who are considered to have mild to moderate disabilities (Skrtic, 1995b). Yet standardized tests continue to be the primary—and, sometimes, the only—means by which students' school performance is measured to ascertain the presence of a so-called "deficit" (McDonnell et al., 1997). For instance, in an analysis of the tools used to assess students' readiness for kindergarten, Cooney (1995) noted that the instruments tended to invalidate the indigenous drawing and storytelling skills of culturally and linguistically diverse students because these skills were not consonant with the schools' expectations for understanding of print concepts and sequential narration. She pointed out that, as a result, "children and their families are blamed for having deficient skills upon school entry" (Cooney, 1995, p. 164). Similarly, many students are classified as having speech and language impairment because of low proficiency in English or because their differences in language patterns are perceived as deficient (Roseberry-McKibbin, 1995; Wolfram, 1992).

The problem with IQ and other standardized tests is that they overlook the fact that children are competent in multiple domains, such as kinesthetic and interpersonal skills, and not just in the academic domains that IQ tests measure (Gardner, 1983; Trawick-Smith, 1997) and that the process of learning is mediated by their environment whereby they exhibit the acquisition of these skills in culturally specific ways (Bérubé, 1996; Serpell, 1994; Trawick-Smith, 1997). A study by Serpell (1994) on the cultural construction of intelligence illustrates dramatically the need to develop alternative means of assessing students' innate skills. Serpell noticed that Zambian students who grew up in an environment in which children's books and crayons were scarce could create quite sophisticated skeletal three-dimensional model cars from scraps of wire, which demonstrated their ability to reproduce patterns, but did less well in a drawing version of the same task. Conversely, English students had no difficulty with copying a two-dimensional picture with pencil and paper but did not perform as well as the Zambian students on the wire-modeling version. What is interesting is that both groups, who were equally familiar with clay, did equally well on the clay-modeling version.

Disability Is a Chronic Illness   Related to the aforementioned beliefs is the assumption that disability is a chronic phenomenon, the Western rationalist dichotomy between spirit and body explains all etiologies of disability in terms of physical or biological dysfunction (Zola, 1986). Furthermore, the Judeo-Christian belief that an individual has only one bodily life on this Earth leads to the interpretation that a chronic condition is permanent rather than temporary. In contrast, for people who believe in reincarnation, for instance, a lifelong condition would be perceived as temporary. Western time is both linear—it runs on and out—and abstract:

> The artifactual time of decontextualized, abstract hours, minutes, and seconds . . . where time is controlled and where it is used as a medium for the translation of labor power into a monetary value . . . is not a human universal. It belongs firmly to the history of Western economic life and paid employment. (Adam, 1995, p. 28)

Although life is predicated on natural (e.g., circadian) time all over the world, this clock time that Adam described forms an integral part of contemporary Western societies' time consciousness. As a finite, measurable resource, it conveys a message of time running out for the human body and death as the final end (Hall, 1983). The concept of time as linear and arbitrarily divided has implications for transition and personal futures planning in special education.

It is on the understanding that a single lifetime is all the clock time that individuals have to maximize their potential that most mainstream families will consider and pursue courses of treatment and interventions to ameliorate the effects of the disability and on which special education and rehabilitation policy is based. In other words, families are more likely to seek help if they think that this lifetime is all the time that they have. An example of this is the notion of transition planning, a legal requirement, which contributes to the popularity of practical tools for personal futures planning. Such approaches are complicated by the fact that there is a discrepancy between institutional transitions, such as graduation from school, on which social policies are constructed, and developmental transitions, such as puberty, on which family life cycles are constructed (Mallory, 1995). As a result, families, including mainstream ones, may find themselves compelled to consider their child's future in terms of an institutional transition before the child may have crossed a corresponding developmental threshold. For instance, many parents express concern about being required by mandate to send their 3-year-old child with disabilities to an educational, non–home-based program, in a transition that they perceive to be neither developmentally appropriate nor culturally normative (V. Turbiville, personal communication, November 22, 1997).

Disability Requires Remediation or "Fixing"   The related fields of special education and rehabilitation are based on the premise that disability is a problem that needs to be and can be "fixed" or remediated. Furthermore, because it is assumed that the disability is intrinsic to the child, interventions are geared exclusively toward remedying this condition within the child, ignoring the impact of environment (Bogdan & Knoll, 1995). Two cornerstone tenets of special education—normalization and behavior modification—emerge from these assumptions. The understanding is that individuals with disabilities can be "normalized" when provided with the repertoire of environments and activities to which typical peers without disabilities would have access and when taught the skills for successful participation through a process of behavior modification. In other words, given the opportunities to the same outcomes of life as their peers without disabilities, individuals with disabilities will have socially valued roles (Wolfensberger, 1972).

The value of equity underlies all policy and practice that justify efforts to remediate or compensate for an individual's disability. It is also the underpinning for ideologies such as mainstreaming or inclusion, which are based on the understanding that the life with the best quality is one that most closely resembles the pattern of lives of peers without disabilities. The intent is to mitigate the inequality that is inherent in this immutable characteristic by mandating and providing accommodations for students with disabilities (Turnbull & Turnbull, 1998).

Contrasting Traditions in Defining Disability

The pivotal role played by the law and professionals in constructing disability that we take for granted in a low-context culture such as the United States is not a universal phenomenon. In high-context cultures, "the meaning of impairment must be understood in terms of cosmology and values and purposes of social life" (Whyte & Ingstad, 1995, p. 10). High-context cultures also lack the level of abstraction and belief in the immutability of science that characterize low-context cultures (Hall, 1981), contributing to an alternative perspective of disability: the social systems perspective (Mercer, 1973), or the community model (Edwards, 1997). In this context, disability has no inherent meaning but is defined by any given community's understanding of people's roles, and the degree to which one is able to fulfill the tasks of membership determines the degree of one's physical ability or disability (Edwards, 1997; Talle, 1995). For instance, although certain descriptors, such as *pêros* ("maimed" in ancient Greece [Edwards, 1997]), "No-Eyes" ("blind" in many American Indian tribes [Locust, 1988]), or *dhegoole* ("without ears" in Somalia [Helander, 1995]), imply a set of conditions, the image intended by the term varies from usage to usage, informed by the context (Edwards, 1997; Talle, 1995), and is not meant to signify the individual as being a member of a category of "disabled people" (Chan, 1986; Helander, 1995; Locust, 1988).

Furthermore, the value that is attached to a specific condition varies among families, in terms of whether it is perceived as disabling and/or stigmatizing. For instance, Joe noted that although many Navajo families would disagree that the professional diagnosis of Down syndrome implicitly connotes a disabling condition because, in their perspective, "the child functions well at home and exhibits no physical evidence of disability . . . [has] all the body parts and in their appropriate places . . . walks, eats, and helps others at home" (1997, p. 254), Navajo families who have high academic expectations for their children would be devastated by the diagnosis. Similarly, among many Hmong families, epilepsy is neither a disability nor stigmatizing but an illness of "some distinction . . . and a sign that the person has been chosen to be the host of a healing spirit" (Fadiman, 1997, p. 21), a position of high social status (Fadiman, 1997).

In this section, we examine four assumptions of the social systems perspective that contrast with those of the medical model:

1. Disability is a spiritual phenomenon.
2. Disability is a group phenomenon.
3. Disability is a time-limited phenomenon.
4. Disability must be accepted.

In noting that the assumptions of the social systems model contrast with those of the positivistic medical model, we are not implying that the former are irrational but that they emerge from a set of values that often are diametrically opposed to those that are embedded in Western rationalist thought. Indeed, there is always a perfectly rational explanation for a belief (Harris, 1974; Kleinman, 1980). For example, the various, seemingly irrational behaviors of many families in most non-Western societies to ensure good health and longevity, including imposing taboos on pregnant woman, conducting naming ceremonies for newborns well after birth when their survival is reasonably assured, and avoiding all actions that might appear to savor of complacence about one's good health, are responses to the scientific reality of high maternal and infant mortality rates. By the same token, rituals such as baby showers and planning the nursery, customary in societies in which the pregnancy is assumed to end in the birth of a healthy child who will grow to become an adult, can be seen as unimaginable, almost irrational behaviors in societies in which such an outcome is not guaranteed.

Disability Is a Spiritual Phenomenon   Adherents to the contrasting or alternative perspective do not necessarily rule out the possibility of a physical etiology to a disability; the difference is that they may also ascribe spiritual or sociocultural causes (Danseco, 1997b; Serpell, Mariga, & Harvey, 1993). For example, many Hmong (Fadiman, 1997; Meyers, 1992), Native American (Locust, 1988), and Pacific Islander (Nicolaisen, 1995) families impute to illness a natural cause, such as the environment, old age, changes in weather, or drinking or eating unsuitable water or food; however, by far the most common cause of illness is soul loss, or "ghost sickness" (Locust, 1988, p. 321). In Fadiman's (1997) study of a Hmong family whose daughter developed epilepsy, the parents attributed the condition, which they referred to as the sickness in which "the spirit catches you and you fall down," to soul loss caused by fright. As Nicolaisen noted,

The distinction between body and soul, and the belief in the volatility and vulnerability of the latter, form the explanatory principles of [Pacific Islanders'] understanding of major congenital handicaps . . . as well as of mental disturbances and a variety of other illnesses. (1995, p. 44)

Similarly, the Mexican American families in Mardiros's (1989) study attributed their child's disability both to biomedical causes, such as chronic health problems during pregnancy or pollution, and to sociocultural beliefs, such as marital difficulties and divine punishment for parental transgressions. Research suggests that deeply religious families (Rogers-Dulan & Blacher, 1995) and families who engage in traditional healing practices (Locust, 1988; Smart & Smart, 1991) are more likely to attribute sociocultural beliefs as a cause of disability than are others.

The "evil eye," curses, and other metaphors of spiritual malevolence also are seen as common causes for sickness and disability among many African (Helander, 1995; Talle, 1995), Hmong (Fadiman, 1997), Jewish Oriental (Stahl, 1991), Native American (Locust, 1988), and Latin American (Groce & Zola, 1993) families. These spiritual concepts have a distinct social component and are believed to have been triggered by some neglected duty or obligation of the victim. In a case in which the victim is a child, the cause may be envy from those less fortunate (Devlieger, 1995; Helander, 1995). As a result, many deem it a bad omen to express admiration for anything good, such as a large and healthy family (Fadiman, 1997; Talle, 1995). This belief in the concept of the "evil eye" has an impact on the families' responses to illness and disability, including beliefs about causes and treatments sought. For example, some Maasai families distinguish between congenital anomalies, which are viewed as being caused by a divine curse—an act of God—and acquired disabilities, which are caused by sorcery—a human act—in response to a social transgression; whereas nothing can be done about the former, the latter condition might be ameliorated through the services of a shaman and/or by righting the wrong (Talle, 1995).

Another spiritual explanation for a disability is that it is direct evidence of a transgression in a previous life of either the parents or the child, a belief strongly held among many Southeast Asian (Chan, 1986; Danseco, 1997b) and Indian (Groce & Zola, 1993) families who believe in reincarnation. To many Mexican American (Smart & Smart, 1991), African American (Rogers-Dulan & Blacher, 1995), and Tswana (Ingstad, 1995) families, their child with disabilities is a gift from God. Among many Songye (Devlieger, 1995) and

Hmong ("Hmong family," 1991) families, a child who is born with certain characteristics sometimes will be considered to be an ancestor who has come back into the family; that is, the child is said to be born with "the spirit of the ancestor" (Devlieger, 1995). For example, in the case of a child who is born with a clubfoot, the Songye interpretation is that the ancestor was not well buried—a coffin was too small and caused the feet to be pressed (Devlieger, 1995). The Hmong interpretation is that the ancestor had been wounded in the foot in a battle ("Hmong family," 1991). Thus, families may have several nonphysical explanations for the causes of disability; this phenomenon has implications for families' help-seeking behavior.

Disability Is a Group Phenomenon   A tacit understanding in all of the nonphysical explanations for the causes of a disability is that the child is not solely responsible for its occurrence but that the entire family is implicated. For instance, many Native American tribes believe that although a spirit may choose to inhabit the body of a person with a disability for some purpose that the spirit and the Supreme Creator have determined, "the causes of a body's being handicapped may lie with the parents (as in the case of fetal alcohol syndrome), and consequently the blame for (prenatal) mutilation of a body falls on the parents" (Locust, 1988, p. 326). Similarly, many Maasai families believe that although the supernatural punishment for an ancestor's sins, such as dereliction of duty to one's parents, comes in the form of the child with a disability, the child itself cannot be blamed for it (Talle, 1995). What is interesting is that although many of the Tswana parents of children with disabilities whom Ingstad (1995) interviewed claimed that their child was a gift from God, or *mpho ya modimo*, even in some cases naming the child Modimo, or God, other families in the community referred to the child as *mopakwane*, a condition believed to be caused by breaking taboos against sexual intercourse during pregnancy; however, this decidedly negative label stigmatized the parents, not the child. Again, among many Songye families, disability is made a relational problem between human beings and the occurrence of disability in the family the starting point for an inquiry into the relations of the family; the assumption is that "the problem of disability is not a problem of the individual but rather a problem of the family" (Devlieger, 1995, pp. 100–101).

There are positive and negative implications for this perspective of group responsibility, however. On one hand, the stigma that is attached to a condition affects the entire family. On the other hand, the stigma is mitigated by a holistic view that interprets disability and illness in terms of family rather than individual traits

(Harry & Kalyanpur, 1994). For example, in Harry's (1992a, 1992d) study, the Puerto Rican American parents tended to describe individual difficulties in terms of a normal range of diversity within the family pattern, allowing for a less stigmatizing interpretation of a child's slowness in reading or a quick temper as being "just like his aunt" or "just like her father." Similarly, many Asian families often interpret their child's school-based difficulties as "laziness," oppositional behavior, or indications that they may not have trained their children adequately (Chan, 1986). Another positive aspect of group responsibility is the collectivistic support that becomes available to the family. For example, Locust noted that

> (American) Indians believe that an individual's spiritual illness can affect the group (family and friends), and thus group efforts are required to return all members of the group to wellness. As a result, students who are not ill may be absent from school in order to assist a sick relative in returning to wellness. Although this group effort is of vital importance to tribal, clan, and family members, it often becomes a point of antagonism between group membership and school officials, resulting in discriminating actions by school authorities. (1988, p. 319)

Disability Is a Time-Limited Phenomenon   Beliefs about the causes of disability can affect a family's perspective on whether a condition is chronic. Among many non-Western cultures, time is cyclical and, therefore, infinite (Fadiman, 1997; "Hmong family," 1991; Locust, 1988; Meyers, 1992). The past, then, is not necessarily that period of time that occurs between an individual's birth to the present moment, as might be understood in most Western cultures, but also the preceding period, which includes previous lives (Fadiman, 1997). Similarly, the future need not be the period between the present and the moment of death but can include the period following the death of the corporal body, wherein the spirit will go on to inhabit yet another body (Locust, 1988). Those who see a spiritual explanation for the disability, such as soul loss, view the child's condition as temporary, with the hope that either the soul would be recalled (Fadiman, 1997) or the child would outgrow the problem (Smith & Ryan, 1987). Danseco noted that among families who believe in reincarnation, "disability is perceived as a temporary condition when viewed along several possible lives" (1997b, p. 44); the disability itself is seen as the result of an event in a previous life. In some cases, this perception also contributes to a sense of fatalism, of acceptance of the disability, as is discussed later.

Furthermore, this notion of cyclical, infinite time has implications for transition and personal futures planning. First, the future is intangible and death is merely a transition into the realm of possibilities for new and unknown lives, making futures planning an exercise in futility. Second, to plan for the future is to assume a certain life expectancy that may be inappropriate, especially for an individual with a disability (Whyte & Ingstad, 1995), or may appear as though one were unappreciative of the present (Brady & Anderson, 1983; Cunningham, Cunningham, & O'Connell, 1986; Locust, 1988). Thus, many families might not have a place for transition planning in their repertoire of needs if they believe that the disability is a temporary condition and that the present is more significant than the future.

Disability Must Be Accepted A family's perceptions of the cause of disability has a great impact on 1) whether they will seek help and 2) the types of interventions that they will seek (Danseco, 1997b). Reasons for accepting the disability are many. For instance, a study of familial attitudes in Africa (Serpell, Mariga, & Harvey, 1993) found that families who attributed a condition to witchcraft, an act of God, or natural causes were likely to seek help, whereas those who linked the condition to family ancestors tended to accept it without seeking external help. Similarly, among many Maasai families, a child with a disability is a fact of life that must be accepted, and statements such as, "We met him just like that" (Talle, 1995, p. 62; referring to a child who was born with a disability), convey the message that the child's impairment is an act of God and is beyond human comprehension and ability to cure. Again, the belief among many Hmong families that the body must be whole to reincarnate as a whole being compels them to reject invasive medical procedures such as surgery, prostheses, dental fillings, and autopsies (Fadiman, 1997; Meyers, 1992). The belief among many Hubeer families that individual deviance is given "cosmological sanction and religious legitimation by the astrological system" (Helander, 1995, p. 75) facilitates a fatalistic acceptance of the disability.

It is important to note, however, that most families do seek intervention; the type of service often depends on what is perceived to be the cause of the disability. For instance, in their study of African families, Serpell et al. (1993) noted that families who attributed a condition to an act of God were more likely to seek help from a modern medical facility, whereas those who believed that witchcraft was involved were as likely to visit traditional practitioners as a medical facility. Similarly, the Hmong family in Fadiman's (1997) study treated their epileptic daughter with the anticonvulsants prescribed by American doctors and a soul-calling ceremony, performed by a shaman, to retrieve the soul. Among Songye families who believe that disability is a response to disharmony in the relationships among family members, the father of the child with the disability may ask his wife to redistribute her bridewealth among the members of the family to restore harmony (Devlieger, 1995). Helander (1995) noted that many Hubeer families initially might seek different medicines or healing techniques, both traditional and modern, but the few, if any, results and the cumulative costs of health care combine to fuel feelings of despair and resignation, at which point the terms *naafo* or *boos* (to mean "hopeless") are used to describe the person to imply that nothing more can be done.

Whether families choose to do nothing or to seek help, their actions are grounded in an acceptance of the disability. Indeed, among many groups, there is little awareness of the potential for rehabilitating, finding roles, or developing adapted life styles for adults with disabilities (Helander, 1995), and the notion that a child with disabilities can be helped by early intervention or stimulation may not be part of common knowledge (Brady & Anderson, 1983; DeGangi, Wietlisbach, & Royeen, 1994) or, in the case of many developing countries, even the standard knowledge base of medical and educational professionals (Groce & Zola, 1993).

One factor that accounts for this level of acceptance is the belief in fate, or "karma" (Danseco, 1997b), which is enhanced when the cause for the disability is perceived to be divine retribution for one's sins. This fatalism has been instrumental in some Christian Scientist families' choosing not to seek medical treatment even for a child with a life-threatening illness (Fadiman, 1997). Another factor is the belief in value inequality, referred to previously, which, in assuming that every individual has his or her own niche within a social hierarchy with its ascribed roles and status, runs counter to the concept of maximization of potential. Attempting to change this status quo by seeking treatment or interventions would be tantamount to destroying the existing social equilibrium and harmony, an act that would affect the entire community ("Hmong family," 1991).

CONCLUSION

This chapter identified the cultural underpinnings of special education policy and professional knowledge. Because the values that underlie policy are congruent with those held by the mainstream culture, most families benefit from the provisions of policy and legal mandate. The conflict arises when families do not subscribe to these same values and yet are required to use services within this framework. Furthermore, professional epistemology is based predominantly on the clinical perspective of the medical model. The assumptions of the medical model—that disability is physical, is chronic, is individually owned, and can be fixed—have serious implications for students from linguistically and culturally diverse backgrounds as well as for families who may believe that disability has spiritual causes, is temporary, is group owned, and must be accepted.

3

The Role of Professional Expertise and Language in the Treatment of Disability

Beth's Story

My introduction to the language of special education in the United States came at a very sensitive period of my life. My 4-month-old daughter, Melanie, had been diagnosed as having incurred brain damage in utero and/or at birth, and I was in the earliest phases of accepting and adjusting to the shock of this event. One of my best friends was coming from Canada to visit, and I sent her the following cable: "Longing to see you. Bring books on brain-injured children and cheese." The displacement of "cheese" in the sentence was intentional; I hoped to amuse my friend, who knew my great love of cheese, while also letting her know of my anxiety over my daughter's condition. My friend understood both my need for new information and for the reassurance that life would still go on as normal. She brought both books and cheese.

I embarked on several months of intensive reading of the current theories and instructional approaches regarding disabilities in young children. I have no idea how much of what I read I absorbed, engrossed as I was in the day-to-day realities of caring for an infant with severe feeding difficulties. What I recall most from that reading was how struck I was by the strangeness of the language. On the level of semantics, there were phrases that were new to me, despite my advanced education in the English language—for example, *multiply handicapped,* which I kept reading as though it were the verb *to multiply* because I had never heard this used as an adjective. The word *label,* which I had never heard used to refer to a classification or a designation of a person, to me really was something that you put on a jar.

On a practical level, the language of the texts that I was reading seemed too technical for a field that I expected to be very personal and humanistic. The phrase *service delivery system* was one that seemed particularly strange. Pausing to think about my discomfort with this phrase, I found that it brought to mind an image of a delivery van doing its rounds. The connotations that went along with this image included a predetermined schedule, neat packages to be dropped off at designated addresses, fixed fees for these services, and uniformed drivers carrying out the simple, clearly specified task of delivering a package on time. I found the image disturbing: Would the delivery van not stop for a while at my home? What if I needed someone to talk to? What if I opened the package and discovered that it wasn't quite what I needed or that I didn't know how to use it? What if I were not home when the van came?

The verbs of the service delivery system were equally disconcerting. Mostly, they seemed to me appropriate to physical or non-human phenomena rather than to the supremely vulnerable children and families with whom the field of special education would have to deal—for example, the word *service* as a verb for providing services related to disability. Until that time, I had heard the verb *service* used to refer only to servicing vehicles or machines. Similarly, the word *measure* connoted for me physical phenomena, which, when related to humans, could refer only to features such as height, weight, blood components, and so forth. Yet I read of researchers who were measuring parents' attitudes and emotions, as well as babies' attachment to their mothers. Furthermore, did *intervene* mean that professionals would move in and take over? Until that time, I had expected that word to be applied mainly to the resolution of disputes by a third party.

Now, more than 20 years later, I am occasionally startled to hear myself using some of these terms. Others are still strange to me; but even when I disagree with the appropriateness of much of the language commonly used within the field, I do understand the reasons for its use. For example, I now see that the use of technological vocabulary and concepts is driven by the field's concern to prove its place in the scientific paradigm from which it claims authority. I understand that credibility resides in the ability to appear objective and that objectivity is taken to mean the documentation of phenomena in ways that make them seem measurable. I believe that the field has sought to apply the goals and methods of the physical sciences to a set of phenomena that are, very often, unmeasurable, such as intelligence, social adaptation, or interpersonal attachment.

Maya and I are not unique in disagreeing profoundly with much of this way of framing disability. Many other scholars have noted its social and political implications and have proposed a social constructionist perspective, which acknowledges the role of human decision making and judgment in the creation of the construct of disability. Yet the categorical language of the special education system continues to predominate in professional circles, and, more important, it continues to be the primary vehicle for communication with the families of children who are designated as having disabilities. Our personal experience and our research have convinced us that whether this language is used deliberately to exclude people who do not share membership in the field or is used unconsciously on the assumption that it is universally comprehensible, it too often functions as a source of alienation and disempowerment for families of children with disabilities.

Language, however, is only one manifestation of the persona of the professional. At the heart of that persona is a simple requirement: To be professional, one must retain an impression of objectivity and factuality. That is not to say that one must be cold or inhuman but that one's reasoning and judgment must be based on evidence that can be demonstrated objectively. In matters of disability, however, the problem is that the evidence is all too often of a subjective, unmeasurable, and socially constructed nature.

This chapter addresses the way in which professional preparation uses the positivist paradigm to develop beliefs, practices, and language that reinforce the impression of objectivity. We discuss these issues in the light of the experiences of parents who come as outsiders into the maze of special education services.

THE CHARGE FOR EXPERT DIAGNOSIS AND TREATMENT

A teacher's role is to teach. This simple truism contains several assumptions (Danseco, 1997a; Harry, Allen, & McLaughlin, 1996; Lightfoot, 1978; Valdés, 1996). First, parents consider themselves responsible for the social and moral development of their children, whereas teachers are expected to be responsible for children's cognitive and academic growth. Second, although these areas of development may overlap somewhat, the teaching occurs in exclusive domains; that is, academic instruction takes place in school, whereas socialization and moral behavior are taught at home. Third, teachers have the expertise to teach, which comes from many years of specialized training; parents lack this expertise because they have not undergone training.

Although this tacit knowledge has been identified primarily within the realm of general education, it is equally relevant to special education. More so, in fact, because professionals in special education are assumed to have the expertise not only to instruct through remediation and other appropriate mechanisms but also to identify the beneficiaries of these specialized services. More so also because professionals in special education are charged by law to undertake this responsibility, and the understanding that professional knowledge will inform these processes is explicit (Turnbull & Turnbull, 1998). Consequently, in the special education arena, this charge establishes a clear hierarchy of knowledge in which professionals' expertise ranks higher than parents'. As in any hierarchy, this creates a certain imbalance of power (Fine, 1993): Professionals have it, parents do not. As Fine (1993) noted, professionals can choose to give parents power by involving them in the education decision-making process, but even this delegation of authority tends to be initiated and controlled by professionals.

The legal mandate for parent participation attempts to restore this power differential caused by the hierarchies of knowledge and, by extension, of status by requiring parental input and parent–professional partnerships in the decision-making process. As this chapter illustrates, however, the issue of power continues to affect families and professionals in the implementation of the mandate.

Expert Knowledge as Categorical and Objective Knowledge

The traditional paradigm of professionalism, what Schön (1983) called *technical rationalism,* has contributed to the implicit assumption that professionals have the expertise to evaluate, classify, and provide appropriate special education services to students who exhibit a specified number of characteristics of a particular disability, an assumption that is further reified under the Individuals with Disabilities Education Act (IDEA) of 1990 (PL 101-476) and its amendments of 1997 (PL 105-17; Skrtic, 1995b). Rooted in positivism, technical rationalism also assumes that the scientific method can be used systematically to accumulate objective knowledge about reality (Skrtic, 1995b).

Objectivity is highly valued in the low-context culture of Western professionalism (Hall, 1981), the assumption being that professionals are likely to diagnose and remediate more effectively when they are not emotionally involved with their clients (Swick, 1997) and when the process is informed by a scientifically based and, therefore, objective body of knowledge that yields universal solutions. Indeed, the concept of objectivity itself is essentially Western (Glasser, 1992; Maruyama, 1983). As Pedersen noted, "Western culture emphasizes objectivity and the scientific method of discovering the truth as more valid and reliable than subjective and spiritual access to knowledge" (1981, p. 324). Objectivity implies a level of decontextualization in that a specific body of knowledge is stripped of its context so that, conversely, it has the same meaning across all contexts. This categorical knowledge, as a universal truth, does not permit the possibility for alternative points of view.

Furthermore, professionals expect and are expected to have a great deal of autonomy in their jobs and to make decisions on the basis of their own professional competence (Heshusius, 1982; Hoberman & Mailick, 1994; Schön, 1983). As Schön (1983) noted, the mechanistic world of the technical rationalist presents professionals with the challenge of maintaining professional distance or objectivity while asking the right questions toward identifying the problem and then providing the answers themselves.

The Language of Objectivity

Beliefs about the objectivity and universality of professional knowledge are reflected in the language that professionals are taught to use. We recognize several positive aspects of this process, including the drive to make language more accountable by systematizing it and the desire to develop language that is respectful of people with disabilities and their families. We believe that as professionals, however, we should develop a critical perspective that will allow us to see the paradoxes in the best of our efforts. We address three aspects of concern in this process.

First, the categorical nature of the labeling and diagnostic process leads to a reifying tendency that is widely known (Bogdan & Knoll, 1995). Once the label has been assigned, it is all too easy to attribute all of the child's difficulties to this presumed fact. This was the process at work when, for example, a professional in Harry's (1992a, 1992d) study of Puerto Rican parents exclaimed impatiently to a parent who wondered whether the instructional practices might account for her child's difficulty in reading: "Well, you see, it's because her disability is in learning to read. That's her disability."

Second, the desire to be seen as a source of objective knowledge often leads professionals to hide behind their jargon. This is particularly disturbing in light of the fact that much of our professional knowledge is ambiguous and impressionistic. The tendency to use jargon as a disguise often is encouraged by our own knowledge that the professional perspective may not be shared by the parent with whom we are communicating. These conflicts can result in situations such as the following, which was reported in Harry, Allen, and McLaughlin's (1995) study of the experiences of a group of African American parents of preschoolers: At an annual review conference, a parent asked the meaning of the term *Level IV,* which, in that state, meant a particular level of service, such as the number of hours, types of services, and so forth. However, the district also used 04 as a code for mental retardation. The parent was told the meaning of Level IV, but noticing the notation *04* on the child's file, the parent went on to say, "Oh, so that's 04." The mistake in interpretation was allowed to pass without correction or clarification by the professional. Because the parent had not asked in which category the child had been classified for special education services, the term *mental retardation* had not been introduced. (This was a strategy noted in annual reviews for children in the 3–6 years age range, where professionals were hesitant to affix a label on such a young child, yet the classification had to be given for services to be received.) The professionals in this case seemed relieved to be able to let the moment pass.

Third, the jargon itself is created by means of strategies that have the effect of excluding or at least confusing outsiders to the field. Some of the most common strategies are what we refer to as the value-neutral or euphemizing process, the abstracting process, and the medicalizing process.

The Value-Neutral or Euphemizing Process   As noted at the beginning of this book, one way to offer an impression of objectivity is to replace words that evoke emotional responses, or subjective judgments, with technical or supposedly value-neutral language. This strategy is not peculiar to special education. We spoke, for example, of the difference between using the word *airplane* as opposed to *equipment.* Ready examples of this process also can be found in books on family life education, where the traditional vernacular words for sexual organs or activities are replaced by medical language. What, for example, might be the difference in effect between the word *womb* as compared with *uterus?* For anyone raised on the Bible, it is likely that *womb* brings to mind "the fruit of thy womb, Jesus," or any other of the widely known biblical stories that refer to the birth process. Thus, the word is likely to have a much more emotional connotation than would the more recent and technical word *uterus*. What might be the difference in effect between using a term such as *self-stimulating sexual behavior* as compared with *masturbation*?

The same process can be seen at work in special education as the field struggles to replace derogatory language with language that is either value neutral or, at best, respectful. Most obvious in this regard are the changes in the terms used to refer to different disabilities. For example, old terms for particular conditions of mental retardation are now not only obsolete but also offensive, such as *mongol, cretin,* and *moron*. These originally were used as technical terms that specified supposedly precise levels or syndromes of mental impairment. Society's abhorrence and consequent rejection of individuals with these conditions, however, resulted in the terms themselves having taken on the unpleasant connotations associated with the people to whom they referred. Replacing these terms with the supposedly neutral term *mental retardation* was an attempt to soften the diagnosis, as the word *retardation* should imply a delay only in mental development. Within a couple of decades, however, the new term had come to reflect the continuing stigma attached to people with the condition, and derogatory terms such as *retard* soon came to serve the same purpose as the old *mongol* or *moron*. The term *handicapped* underwent the same fate, and many professionals prefer the term *challenged*, whether physically or mentally.

An interesting by-product of the labeling process is its potential for backlash by the people to whom the labels refer. Usually, terms that describe marginalized individuals or groups are assigned to them by the mainstream, not by the people themselves. As the society becomes aware of its prejudice against such people, it struggles to soften its perspective by using language that it hopes is more technical or less value laden. Often, however, the recipients of the terminology come to a point at which they begin to resent and ultimately reject being described as *other* and seek their own redefinitions. Often, their solution is to return to the traditional, stigmatizing language in an effort to reclaim and redefine the marginalized identity. The Black power movement is a prime example of this, whereby the previously stigmatizing term *Black* became the rallying cry of the reclamation of identity. Although many have since come to prefer the term *African American*—another step toward reclaiming a long-devalued history—many Black youth have taken the ultimate step: using the term *nigger* as their way of throwing in the face of society its own prejudice while restating a pride in all that had previously been reviled by whites (Logan, 1996). The term *Indian* has undergone the same process, in place of the mainstream's *Native American* (Red Horse, 1988). In the field of disability, the same has been true of the Deaf community, for whom the term *deaf* is used to emphasize deafness as something of which to be proud (Livingston, 1997).

Another way of neutralizing language is to borrow words from technical activities, thereby emphasizing the mechanistic and more systematic aspects of a process. For example, the word *service,* when used as a noun, loses all of its traditional connotations of something offered through serving, which is further underscored by the use of the same word as a verb, which traditionally referred to the maintenance or repair of a machine. Thus, we hear early interventionists speaking of "servicing" a family. By contrast, the word *serve,* which is the source of all of these terms, seldom is used, and then only by someone who wants to emphasize that professional efforts ought to focus on humanistic or altruistic practice.

Another technical term is the word *system,* which, as was commented on in the opening anecdote to this chapter, when paired with *service,* connotes a level of mechanistic practice that really is neither desirable nor feasible. Even the term *family system,* although intended to emphasize the interconnectedness of family members and functions, also has the effect of understating the very human unpredictability that so often confounds professionals' best attempts at prediction and planning.

This is the main point about the borrowing of technical terms: Its purpose is to make our activities sound more systematic and more objective, while, in reality, they continue to be marked by human ambiguity and often are driven more by intuition than by reason. But human judgment is just that—judgment—and the discrepancy between the ideal of objectivity and the reality of subjectivity results in the undermining of our confidence in our ability to make true professional judgments.

The Abstracting Process   Another strategy is to use language that effectively abstracts the essential properties of a range of materials or activities so as to be able to refer to general categories without specifying individual items. This process results in some words that are tremendous favorites of teachers, such as *manipulatives*—a sensible word that can include a wide array of toys, learning materials, and miscellaneous items but that carries no meaning for most parents. Another version of this is the use of words that refer to processes or services that are universally recognized by professionals but that may be unknown to the uninitiated. The most common of these tend to be acronyms, such as *IEP, OT, PT, SLP,* and so forth. Although the goal of this process is to establish a universal, shared meaning that all professionals inducted into the culture of special education can recognize, local variations in terminology can defeat this effort: In Florida, for example, the term *staffing* refers to the process of meeting and making decisions about a child's placement. Thus, "staffings" are routinely held for the purpose of children's being "staffed in" or "staffed out" of special education services. Of course, it seems ironic that the term reflects a focus on the professionals in the process rather than on the child.

The Medicalizing Process   The attempt to make language seem objective is perhaps most evident in the use of jargon that originates in the fields of medicine and physical sciences. For example, where, in the past, teachers might comfortably have used terms such as *hearing/listening* or *looking/seeing,* words such as *auditory, visual,* or *perceptual* now are among common professional usage and student teachers quickly learn how to use them. It may be that professionals may prefer using these terms because of their greater precision in identifying a specific physiological process rather than a social activity, but they are preferred also because using these words avoids referring to the person who is doing the action. For example, we can see the difference between saying, "He doesn't hear very well," as compared with, "He has difficulties in auditory reception." By taking the actor out of the equation, the sense of objectivity and factuality is increased because interpretations of whether the person was listening, whether the language spoken was appropriate, and so forth would have been ruled out. Thus, it would be assumed that any observer would come to the same conclusion.

Expert knowledge and the language used to convey this knowledge, then, is marked by its objectivity and universality. By the same logic, the experts are those who have acquired this knowledge—that is, the professionals.

The Training of Experts

How do professionals acquire objective and universally applicable knowledge? To ensure that professionals have the competence to diagnose and remediate, they are socialized through a process of training or professional education that is directed toward helping participants acquire these special competencies (Hoberman & Mailick, 1994). The understanding is that members of a profession form a community with similar education, training, and practices as well as commonalities in culture, tradition, language, and qualifications, which are in large part a consequence of their professional education (Skrtic, 1995a). As Skrtic (1995a) pointed out, however, this process of induction has two major flaws. First, it assumes that the body of knowledge that is imparted to students in training is objective because its scientific base renders it value neutral and of universal applicability. Second, it does not permit opportunities for inductees to question the objectivity of the knowledge that they receive and identify the values that, in reality, undergird it. Indeed, Jacob noted,

> Many of the values and concepts promoted in schools and teacher preparation programs are so deeply embedded culturally that they operate without our conscious awareness. Facing and accepting the reality that specific assumptions or values are not universally true can be very threatening. (1995, p. 453)

For instance, many professionals may question why the parents who belong to the same social class as themselves are also the parents whom they are "most comfortable with" and who are the "easiest to work with," whereas the parents who belong to a different social class are the ones whom they find more "difficult to work with" (Dinnebeil & Rule, 1994). Those who do ponder the point might recognize the discrepancies between the assumption of universal applicability embedded in their professional training and the reality of social class differences. For example, some early intervention professionals, who assume that their knowledge is universal, might focus on educating families about development and sharing observations and concerns about the child; the family, conversely, might have very different concepts of child development and of the need for early intervention (DeGangi, Wietlisbach, & Royeen, 1994; Miles & Miles, 1993).

Indeed, professionals are trained to believe that professional knowledge, because it is objective, is akin to the "truth" and that, in the hierarchy of knowledge, it carries greater authority over parents' everyday knowledge of their child, because the latter is subjective and personal.

Ensuring Accountability

Recognizing the potential detrimental effect of cultural bias in the process of diagnosis, the law calls for assessment to be provided by highly trained specialists whose expert use of validated tools ensures the objectivity of the process (Turnbull & Turnbull, 1998). Were the process of evaluation to lead to a status-enhancing outcome, it is extremely likely that few would complain about the event. But the facts are that placement in special education is stigmatizing, that often the labels stay with students throughout their academic lifetime or even beyond, that the instruction that students receive in special education keeps them excluded from general education, and, probably most troubling of all, that students from culturally and linguistically diverse backgrounds and of low-income status tend to end up in special education more than any other group of students (Harry, 1994; Harry & Anderson, 1994; Heller, Holtzman, & Messick, 1982; McDonnell, McLaughlin, & Morison, 1997).

The policy to involve parents in this process, then, is an effort toward restitution and professional accountability (Turnbull & Turnbull, 1998). The intention is twofold. First is the hope that involving parents will elicit alternative perspectives on students' abilities and performance, thus reducing the chances of professional misdiagnosis. Second is to ensure that students who do need remediation will receive, through the advocacy efforts of their parents, an education that is neither inferior in quality nor inappropriate.

It is significant that the onus for informing parents and ensuring their participation is on professionals, although parents also may choose to initiate and sustain their advocacy efforts. As a result, professionals are caught in a web of traditional notions of objective knowledge with themselves as experts, and a contradictory mandate to invite the input of parents whose knowledge of their child is presumed to be unscientific because it is subjective.

THE CONFLICT OF EGALITARIANISM AND EXPERTISM

As Fine asserted, the issue is about "(ap)parent power" (1993, p. 682). The mandate for parent participation directly contravenes the traditional notion of the professional as expert and attempts to overturn the balance of power in favor of parents by its recommendation that parental input about a child be taken into account in the decision-making process. Professionals, trained to believe that their knowledge gives them authority to make decisions about a student's education, must now grapple with the seemingly radical idea that parents can be experts, too.

From the point of view of parents, the conflict is even more bewildering. Many people from nonmainstream cultures tend to view experts as the source of unquestionable knowledge and therefore expect professional expertise to be delivered in a categorical manner (Correa, 1989; Cunningham, Cunningham, & O'Connell, 1986;

Lynch & Stein, 1987). They do not expect to be collaborators or decision makers in the process (Cloud, 1993; Rhodes, 1996) and may neither offer their input, even when solicited, nor disagree with professionals' recommendations (Kalyanpur & Rao, 1991). What results, as this section describes, is considerable miscommunication as professionals attempt to convey professional knowledge to parents while, in turn, parents struggle to acquire professional knowledge.

Egalitarianism and American Professionals

On the basis of the common law doctrine that parents have both a duty to support their children and rights that they can exercise on behalf of their children, IDEA gives parents the right to exercise their child's right to have an education (Turnbull & Turnbull, 1998). IDEA's regulations require state and local education agencies to establish procedures for the participation and consultation with people who are concerned with the education of children with disabilities, including the students themselves and their parents or guardians. Parents must be informed and their consent must be obtained for preplacement evaluation, initial placement of their child in a special education program, and reevaluations. What is most significant is that it is the responsibility of the local education agency to inform parents of the procedural safeguards and their rights pertaining to their child's education. Parents have access to students and system records, as well as the right to confidentiality of students' records. School districts must notify parents when personally identifiable information is on record, and parents have the right to inspect these records and challenge the contents.

Implicit in these requirements are three taken-for-granted beliefs. First is that parents have the right to know; that is, they are equally entitled to have access to the same knowledge about their child as professionals have. Second is that parents will advocate for their child by exercising these rights and by demanding redress should these rights be violated. Third is that all parents are equally knowledgeable and have a "shared understanding" (Harry, 1992b) about the first two beliefs.

As several scholars have noted (e.g., Bowers, 1984; Coots, 1998; Harry et al., 1995, 1996; Lareau & Shumar, 1996; Leon, 1996; Serpell, 1997), however, a significant difference in middle-income and low-income parents' advocacy efforts is that low-income and/or culturally diverse families often do not have this shared understanding about the system, and they may not have the means to learn. Apple and Beane (1995) referred to the acquisition of the tools for success in the mainstream as "cultural capital," or, as Bowers put it, the "knowledge of relevant issues and conceptual frameworks of a culture that enable individuals to successfully negotiate themselves within it" (1984, p. 2). Members of the culture acquire this knowledge "from infancy to adulthood, continuously and effortlessly" (Bowers, 1984, p. 33) without being consciously aware of it, as part of their socialization into the culture. For outsiders to the culture, however, this knowledge has to be learned as a conscious process at the point and time of contact—and, indeed, many may never acquire it. Bowers noted, for example, that an individual who has no knowledge of the tacit assumptions that are embedded in political ideas, such as the Bill of Rights,

> Is not likely to possess a set of taken-for-granted beliefs pertaining to the importance of maintaining civil liberties. . . . The lack of knowledge and exposure to the collective traditions that enable an individual to share in the collective memory will not lead to the individual being influenced by the authority of this area of the culture. (1984, p. 6)

With professionals socialized into the culture of special education, which, in turn, is based on the values of the dominant mainstream culture, it is hardly surprising, then, that many professionals find mainstream (i.e., Anglo American, middle-income) families "easier to work with" (Dinnebeil & Rule, 1994). Where there is this "intimate culture" (Serpell, 1997, p. 589) of tacit understanding about family values, professionals do not expect to or need to explain their practice.

Given the tradition of technical rationalism, most professionals do not expect to explain their practice to families who do not participate in this shared understanding either. On the contrary, historically, parents have been expected to attempt an understanding, however rudimentary, of the professionals' culture (Correa, 1989). As Mlawer (1993) asked, how fair is this advocacy expectation? For instance, a comparative study of the advocacy efforts of parents of high and low incomes with children in special education (Coots, 1998) found that mothers with high-income ratings were able to "customize" their child's schooling if it did not meet the child's needs, for instance, by engaging a phonics tutor to teach a child whom the school had deemed unable to read phonetically. Conversely, mothers with low-income ratings did not take action to find additional services to meet these needs but kept pushing the school to meet the needs; as a result, their child continued to receive inadequate services and they were labeled "difficult" or "noncompliant" parents. In a similar study (Fine, 1993) of parents of children in general education, the low-income mothers did not have access to the elaborate networks of support and information that prevailed among the high-income mothers. Common avenues of access to the school authorities—for instance, by becoming a volunteer in the classroom or a member of the PTA—were, in effect, not available to the low-income mothers because most of them worked outside the home.

Professional compliance without meaningful communication negatively affects all families, including those who have access to the "intimate culture" of the professionals, those who have access to the information and resources that allows them to customize their child's education to meet his or her needs, and those who are aware of their rights and of the avenues for participation and for redress. We assert that the pattern of discourse needs to be changed. Compliance is adequate, although barely so, for middle-income families: If they receive written notice, then they can read and understand its content and then act on it. Most professionals are trained to believe that this pattern of discourse, because it is objective and universalistic, is good professional behavior and that parents are receiving quality service (Fadiman, 1997).

Consider, then, the implications of this pattern of discourse for families who lack this cultural capital. For instance, many Hispanic migrant families do not attend parent meetings because they have limited communication skills or believe that they will not make a difference if they complain (Leon, 1996; Rhodes, 1996); some even fear that if they complain, then the teachers and the system will retaliate by suspending their children (Leon, 1996). Similarly, in Harry's study, professionals could not understand why the Puerto Rican American parents would agree to everything at the meetings, and "then they would go away and say they did not like the decisions that were made" (1992b, p. 480); the parents, on their part, found it difficult to disagree openly or challenge the professionals because of a deep-rooted deference toward teachers.

During her efforts to promote parental involvement in their middle-school child's education and prevent school dropout, Garlington (1991) noticed that many of the inner-city African American parents were not aware that they could call a meeting with their child's teacher if they had a concern. Those who were aware of this avenue hesitated to do so and often put off calling a meeting, however serious the concern might be, because of their history of poor communication with teachers. As a result, concerns that might have been dealt with at early stages often were not addressed until they became serious enough to merit the school's attention.

The advocacy expectation makes assumptions about parents' knowledge of taken-for-granted beliefs about American culture and the special education culture in particular. Parents who lack this shared understanding are at a disadvantage despite the legal mandate for informing parents.

The Professional as a Parent

Historically, information about parents' perspectives on the experiences of having a child with a disability was presented by researchers and professionals who were not themselves parents of children with disabilities (for a review, see Turnbull & Turnbull, 1997). Much of their analysis resulted in a theory of pathology and deficit model of families. For instance, having a child with a disability was assumed to be a burden with few positive outcomes for the family.

The induction of parents into the ranks of professionals contributed considerably to a change in these traditional perspectives. Research on parents conducted by professionals who are themselves parents of children with disabilities (e.g., Behr & Murphy, 1993; Ferguson, Ferguson, & Jones, 1988; Harry, 1992a; Turnbull & Turnbull, 1997) as well as first-person accounts by parents (e.g., Bérubé, 1996; Maurice, 1994; Park, 1982) helped to shape new theories of resilience and strengths-based models of families and affected some of the perceptions about professional knowledge and objectivity.

In response to this growing realization that every person brings to a situation a different point of view, as well as an increasing demand for relevance over rigor, professional education began to acknowledge the impact of individuals' cultural and ethical values on their ability to make professional decisions and the significance of diverse points of view in the development of professional knowledge (Burian & Slimp, 1994; Dukerich, Dutton, & McCabe, 1994; Friedsam, 1995; Maruyama, 1983). This recognition that professionals may have experienced circumstances similar to their clients', indeed have "walked in their clients' shoes" (Burian & Slimp, 1994, p. 40), was a big step away from the objective stance of professionalism.

For many parents, the decision to become a professional is motivated by the need to gain knowledge about the system (Traustadottir, 1995) and often does result in familiarity with professional knowledge such as the terminology of the field, availability of service options, and current professional practices. Although this does not necessarily change the status differential and many professional parents continue to experience "a feeling of dread" about approaching conferences with professionals (M.J. Blue-Banning, personal communication, April 14, 1998), becoming a professional is an option that is available primarily to middle-income families (Carpenter, 1997).

Although many families may be denied the opportunity to become professionals for economic reasons, other parents' opportunity to become professionals may be tied to the issue of equity because becoming a professional means putting oneself on a par with professionals. For middle-income parents, who in other spheres of life may already enjoy professional status, this may not be as much of a leap as it might be for low-income parents. For culturally diverse parents who believe professionals to be authority figures, any effort to place oneself on an equal footing with a professional would smack of extreme conceit and disrespect.

Finally, the experience of being a parent of a child with a disability does not necessarily signify that an individual may relate to all families who have a child with a disability. Indeed, the process of socialization into the profession (Skrtic, 1995b) and individual cultural and ethical values (Dinnebeil & Rule, 1994) can become barriers to collaboration even for those who have had the parental experience firsthand.

Scientific Knowledge versus Everyday Knowledge

Besides ensuring parents' right to have access to professional knowledge, IDEA also seeks to include parents' knowledge about their child to reduce the field's excessive emphasis on professional knowledge with regard to diagnosis and remediation. Despite these legal efforts to balance the power differential, professional expertise in assessment continues to carry greater clout because it is based on a sequence of evaluation tools that are assumed to be scientifically based and therefore objective, whereas parents' everyday knowledge about their child's difficulties traditionally has tended to be dismissed as subjective and anecdotal (Turnbull & Turnbull, 1997). It is no wonder, then, that parent–professional collaboration is so inordinately difficult to accomplish: The ideal of parent participation is based on the macrocultural value of equity and participatory democracy, whereas the ideal of professional as expert is based on the "bureaucratic ranking system" (Hall, 1981, p. 21) of the microculture of special education.

For instance, when Bérubé (1996) "politely" gave the audiologist three valid reasons for why the results of a hearing test for his son might be inaccurate—Jamie would have responded more often to the familiar voices of his parents than to the unfamiliar audiologist's, he would have responded to being called "Jamie" rather than "James," and he turned more often to see the animal move when the audiologist spoke than in response to the sound of her voice—the professionals reacted in the following manner:

> They were understanding. After all, Pt. [patient] was so young, it was difficult to read his responses, and we'd know better in 3 months or so. They were also quite sure that he had a pretty serious hearing loss and that I wouldn't help anything by pretending it wasn't there. They said so very politely, too. (Bérubé, 1996, p. 131)

The professionals' response to Bérubé's objection to the results of the test is representative of the dominant positivistic paradigm and the belief that a validated evaluation instrument has universal applicability because it is objective. Similarly, the suggestion that Bérubé was "in denial" is also fairly typical of the dominant pathology model that imputes deficits in families and individuals with disabilities (Bogdan & Knoll, 1995); as a result, his everyday knowledge about his child's actual skills and hearing ability is dismissed because it is subjective.

When parents from culturally diverse or low socioeconomic backgrounds are involved, the impact of this deficit model is heightened in that the child's culture itself is seen as somehow being at fault, as this comment by a low-income, African American mother about her young son's evaluation reveals:

> She is judging *me*. I met this lady once, *one time,* and she judged me. . . . She kept saying his environment is making him act like that. [But] I am his environment. So what is she trying to say? That I am not a good mother or something? (Kalyanpur & Rao, 1991, p. 527; italics in original)

What, asked Correa, is the message being conveyed when a professional tells a young Hispanic mother that she must "be a good mother and talk to her child" (1992, p. 6)? Similarly, Markey (1997), an African American mother, wondered whether the psychologist who was examining her son with autism recognized the deeper cultural implications of questions such as, "What do fathers do?" and, "Do you like policemen?" Again, in Kalyanpur's study, the professional identified a language delay in the bilingual Native American children because she had observed that they did not engage in much verbal interaction with their mothers, and she concluded that "their culture was hurting them" (1998, p. 322). Finally, Valdés's study powerfully illustrates how the cultural deficit model creates a discrepancy between Mexican American immigrant families' and the mainstream teachers' understanding of parent involvement in their child's education:

> When American teachers expected that Mexican working-class mothers would "help" their children with their schoolwork, they were making assumptions about abilities that the mothers did not have. Moreover, they were also making assumptions about the universality of what, in American schools, counts as knowledge. . . . The parents were not aware that for many teachers, knowing the alphabet was an indicator of children's abilities and of parents' "involvement" in their education. By not making certain that their children arrived in school with the "right" knowledge, they were, in fact, condemning their children to placement in the lowest reading groups. (1996, pp. 166–167)

What often is overlooked is that parents with very little education can be very insightful concerning their child's difficulties. For instance, Harry's (1992a, 1992d) study of the views of low-income Puerto Rican American parents demonstrated that despite limited education, the parents' theories paralleled three arguments that are current among scholars in the field: 1) Labeling is detrimental to children, 2) special education curriculum frequently is repetitive and infantile, and 3) their children's difficulties were attributable to the difficulties involved in acquiring a second language rather than from any intrinsic learning deficits.

Operating within a system that is hierarchical, parents from culturally diverse or low socioeconomic backgrounds are at a double disadvantage because of their societal status and restricted economic choices (Harry, 1992b; Lareau & Shumar, 1996). As Harry noted,

> Parents who do not believe that they can challenge school authorities are likely to withdraw from participation. Out of a traditional respect for authority, however, they may continue to defer to professionals yet fail to cooperate with professional recommendations or even to respond to invitations to participate. (1992b, p. 475)

For instance, Joe noted that many Native American families, "aware that mainstream society has the power to determine what resources will be made available to those with disabilities and by whom" (1997, p. 253), will quietly refuse services or withdraw from interaction with the agencies when faced with a conflict. Studies indicate that this practice of agreeing and "then going away and saying they do not like the decisions that were made" (Harry, 1992b,

p. 480) frustrates many professionals and often leads to misunderstanding (Bernheimer & Keogh, 1995; DeGangi et al., 1994; Harry, 1992b, 1992e; Harry et al., 1995) and, in some instances, to parents' being labeled "noncompliant"—a term, asserted Fadiman, that implies "moral hegemony" (1997, p. 260) and coercion rather than mediation.

In her study of the collision of two cultures, that of a Hmong child with epilepsy and her American doctors, Fadiman (1997) noted that, to the doctors, modern medicine was the "truth" that needed no explanation and provided only one explanation for the condition. Indeed, had the family been comfortable with the culture of modern medicine, they would have needed no explanations. For instance, a middle-income Anglo American family is more likely to be fully conversant and literate in English; to understand complicated instructions about medications and side effects; and to believe in the healing effects of drugs, invasive surgical procedures, and that epilepsy is caused by—and only by—neurochemical imbalances in the brain. In the Hmong family's case, however, the very complex regimen of drugs prescribed did not take into account two significant factors: 1) The family attributed the condition to a spiritual cause, which they believed required a mixture of treatments involving both modern medicine and traditional healing; and 2) the parents' inability to speak, read, or write English prevented them from telling the doctors this. As a result, when the parents stopped administering the drugs, they were viewed as being noncompliant rather than, perhaps, as getting a second opinion or pursuing alternative treatments. On the physicians' recommendation, the child was removed from her family and placed in foster care. (An ironic comment on the state of communication that existed is that although almost the entire Hmong community knew of the child's removal, almost none of the other physicians in the hospital did.)

Despite the legal requirement for eliciting parental input in the education decision-making process, the greater weight that is given to professional expertise in the hierarchy of knowledge skews the balance of power against parents. As a result, parents are expected to know and understand what professionals know, such as the meaning of a diagnosis or a placement. They also are expected to know how to gain access to this knowledge—for instance, by exercising their right to be informed. However, many parents may be denied access to professional knowledge because of a lack of cultural capital and a lack of awareness of this advocacy expectation. Furthermore, families whose cultural beliefs offer opposing points of view are more likely to be perceived as deviant or defiant than different, whereas families from low socioeconomic backgrounds who have limited resources are unfairly situated in a structure that is weighted heavily in favor of professional access to resources.

EQUITY VERSUS HIERARCHY IN THE STRUCTURING OF PARENT–PROFESSIONAL COMMUNICATION

The tension between the requirement for equitable participation and the prevailing hierarchical structure that emerges from the positivist paradigm is also felt in the status that parents are accorded in the decision-making process and the patterns of communication between parents and professionals in formal conferences.

The Mandate of the Law Regarding Parental Participation

In the interests of participatory democracy—that is, the political opportunity of those affected by a public agency's decisions to participate in making those decisions—IDEA provides for shared decision making between parents and professionals (Marshall, Mitchell, & Wirt, 1989; Turnbull & Turnbull, 1998). This vision of parents as collaborators was reaffirmed in the reauthorization of and amendments to IDEA in 1997 (PL 105-17; Turnbull & Turnbull, 1997).

The primary forum for such parent–professional partnerships is the individualized education program (IEP) meeting, the formal conference in which an IEP is developed from both parental and professional input. As Turnbull and Turnbull noted, because parent participation in the student's education is a "high priority" under IDEA, local education agencies are required to take specified steps to ensure that one or both parents are present at the IEP meeting, including "advance notice of the meeting, mutually convenient scheduling of the meeting, and arranging for interpreters for deaf or non–English-speaking parents" (1998, p. 145). Only when efforts to have parents attend have been unsuccessful can the meeting be held without them. Schools must give parents a copy of the IEP if they ask for it. Thus, the law provides opportunities to facilitate parent participation and shared decision making. Again, however, in reality, the implementation of the mandate falls far short of the vision of collaboration and participatory democracy.

Implementation of the Mandate

As discussed in Chapter 2, the legal fiat that requires professionals to collaborate with parents emerges from the ideal of participatory democracy and equity, both central values in the dominant mainstream culture. This is also reflected in the climate of school reform that has contributed to the movement for a restructuring of parent involvement in general education (Fine, 1993).

Ware (1994) pointed out, however, that these reforms have not affected the prevailing model of professionalism that values professional autonomy and hierarchical authority, both barriers that remain significant impediments to collaboration. She asserted that the expectation of autonomy leads more to professional compartmentalization than to interdisciplinary interdependence and shared responsibility with parents. Similarly, centralized power structures traditionally have denied parents' roles outside of their participation in children's homework and parent–teacher conferences and in school events such as open house and fund-raisers, where the agenda and limits of participation are clearly delineated by the professionals (Fine, 1993; Ware, 1994). In the special education system, these barriers are exacerbated by the medical model, which reifies the notion of professional as expert (Harry, 1992b; Skrtic, 1995b; Ware, 1994).

Ware's (1994) argument is underscored by the accounts of parents' unhappy experiences with the special education system. As one mother noted, "Sometimes it appears that [the school personnel] want you so frustrated that you just say 'fine'" (Coots, 1998, p. 513). Furthermore, the societal status of low-income, culturally diverse parents often determines the way parents are treated. For instance, Garlington (1991) noted that as the African American director of an inner-city community outreach project, she was ushered in to administrators' offices upon arrival while the low-income African American parents with whom she worked were kept waiting in the hallways. Similarly, a low-income mother in Coots's study reported that her child's teacher was always "too busy to talk with her" (1998, p. 513).

The low-context, bureaucratic, and hierarchical structure of schools also has an impact on school personnel's efforts to comply with legal requirements to inform parents fully in writing or another suitable manner of communication, in their native language, of any school-initiated special education decisions. Often, compliance becomes an end in itself rather than a means for facilitating communication and shared decision making with parents. For instance, although the responsibility for giving notice to parents lies with the school district, the burden rests on parents to make sure that they have understood the notice (Turnbull & Turnbull, 1998); in other words, if the information was clearly stated, according to the law, then the school has complied, even if the parent does not understand it.

Accustomed as we are to the bureaucratic, legalistic phrase "notice given in writing," it is easy to overlook the cultural assumptions that are embedded in it. First, there is the assumption of literacy. In a country where a majority of the population is literate, indeed where illiteracy is stigmatized, ubiquitous reliance on the written word for communication is a natural outcome, to the point that even informal, everyday situations, such as learning how to open a milk carton or filling up the gasoline tank in one's car, require a certain level of reading skill. The reason, and this leads to the second assumption, is that, as Hall (1981) noted, in low-context cultures, most transactions are mechanistic and decontextualized—acquiring the milk or gasoline, for instance, can be accomplished with a minimum of personal interaction—because it maximizes efficiency. As a result, information is communicated in similarly mechanistic and impersonal ways. Indeed, using low-context, written formats to communicate information about an issue as personal as the educational well-being of children would not be considered inappropriate.

This "highly rational, efficient, 'quick-fix' approach" (McGowan, 1988, p. 62) to communication can be disconcerting to people who are accustomed to a slower, more personal, yet more generalized approach. The dominant value behind the latter approach is the kind of personalism that has been identified as central to high-context cultures. Personalism brings to communication a holistic, relational perspective (Falicov, 1996; Korin, 1996) that increases considerably the significance of contextual details, such as the status of both listener and speaker, and assumes a high level of tacit understanding. Because the focus is more person centered than task centered, the rules of communication often require a more indirect style that would include, for instance, discussion of seemingly tangential issues before coming to the topic at hand (Kalyanpur & Rao, 1991) and the use of allusions, parables, or proverbs to convey an opinion (Falicov, 1996). McKenzie-Pollock gave a good example of what intervention that is based on personalism would look like:

> I once asked a Cambodian teacher for advice about the most effective way to intervene in a case where teachers were referring a child who had talked about domestic violence. She said she would handle this situation by visiting the couple with a gift of food. She would sit with them and chat about family life and values without mentioning the reports of violence. Therefore, the couple would not be shamed by having the problem named, but they would get the message that there was a problem with their or his behavior. (1996, p. 308)

In contrast, the low-context culture of the special education bureaucratic machinery provides parents with written information on
the assumptions that 1) they are literate, 2) a written document is
the most appropriate means of communication, and 3) they will understand the contents of such a decontextualized message. Indeed, a
study of parents' preferences and priorities for receiving information about challenging behaviors (Turnbull & Ruef, 1996) found that
the well-educated, Caucasian mothers chose printed material over
other formats such as audiocassette, videocassette, or parent match-
ing. However, a disproportionate number of people with low levels
of literacy are members of minority groups and/or of low socioeconomic status (Weiss & Coyne, 1997), many of whom are likely to
have children who are at risk for academic failure and are, therefore, likely to receive written notices to this effect. Furthermore,
typical handouts used to inform individuals about their rights are
written at the tenth-grade level or higher, whereas most of the recipients of these documents might be, at best, at third- or fourth-grade
reading levels (Roit & Prohl, 1984; Weiss & Coyne, 1997). For instance, the modern Hmong script was developed in the mid-1950s
(Fadiman, 1997). As a result, illiteracy is common among many
Hmong families:

> To the Hmong, the numerous consent forms, individualized education
> plans or individualized family service plans, and permission forms
> that parents must sign when their child is in an early intervention pro-
> gram are alien and overwhelming. Illiteracy in Hmong or English or
> both further complicates the process of written documentation re-
> quired by local, state, and federal mandates, even though English forms
> may be translated to the Hmong language. (Meyers, 1992, p. 741)

Various sources have suggested that many culturally diverse
and low-income families are more comfortable with alternative formats to written communication (Brady & Anderson, 1983; Meyers,
1992; Pacer Center, 1992a, 1992b; Weiss & Coyne, 1997). These formats include direct communication by telephone or in person
through an interpreter and nonwritten materials, such as picture
books, slide or tape presentations, audiotapes, videotapes, and
models. Indeed, efforts to elicit and respond to parents' needs and
preferences by using a combination of formats have been found to
lead to increased knowledge among all families, both those with
limited literacy and those with good reading skills (Weiss & Coyne,
1997).

For parents who prefer high-context communication, such as
face-to-face contact, a written document also represents the formal,

impersonal style of low-context communication (Hall, 1981). As a result, school districts' preference for written communication often leads to a sense of alienation and powerlessness (Blue-Banning, 1997; Harry, 1992a, 1992c; Harry et al., 1995). For instance, in Harry's (1992a, 1992c) study, the Puerto Rican American families began to lose trust in the school authorities, who consistently sent notices home in compliance with the law but made little effort to develop personal, caring relationships toward more effective communication. One mother had been sent so many letters that, in annoyance, she took the "mountain of papers" to the local Latino center to be stored, an action that she may have been less likely to take had she understood the content and purpose of these papers. The letters also were seen by some parents as somehow threatening because they signified the formal power of the authorities, which would be beyond the parents' power to challenge.

Even when parents can read the document, there often is an absence of meaning (Harry, 1992c; Valdés, 1996). Although parents are fully aware of the significance of a letter from school—indeed, immediately assuming that it means bad news, as Garlington (1991) wryly commented—they may not be familiar enough with the technical language to decipher its meaning (Garlington, 1991; Harry, 1992c). For instance, Harry (1992a, 1992c) noted that two Puerto Rican American parents in her study did not know that their children had been moved from their current placement, although they had received a letter informing them about it. In one case, the letter may have been sent, but the school district acknowledged that it had never been signed by the parent; possibly, they had read the letter but not understood its message. Similarly, only when the meaning of the report cards that were sent home was explained to inner-city African American (Garlington, 1991) and newly immigrated Mexican American (Valdés, 1996) parents—that is, when parents understood what the letter grades stood for and how their children's grades had improved or fallen over a period—were they able to recognize the possibility of their child's dropping out or becoming at risk for academic failure.

When school districts consider a task completed because they have sent the proper documents to parents in compliance with statutory regulations, they overlook the purpose of the task. We can assume that the original intention behind requiring school districts to send certain documents to parents is to 1) inform parents, 2) establish an avenue of communication between parent and professional, and 3) facilitate parents' participation because they have learned from the letter what professionals know about their child and they know what they need to do in response. When parents can neither read nor comprehend the contents of the message, however, this purpose is not served.

The next section examines the imbalance of power and status in the IEP meeting and its implications for parents who may have differing interpersonal communication styles.

The Reality of the IEP Meeting

The very word *meeting* conveys a level of formality that makes many parents uncomfortable (Garlington, 1991). The IEP meeting, with its myriad manifestations of the status differential, is characterized by a low-context–based formality that often results in high levels of discomfort for both parents and professionals and very little communication. For instance, for parents who are accustomed to schools in which teachers have close, caring relationships with students (Harry, 1992c; McKenzie-Pollock, 1996), the formal structure of the IEP meeting is an alienating extension of an impersonal school system.

The paradox between the values of equity and hierarchy becomes apparent once again. For instance, professional efforts to infuse a more egalitarian format into the formal structure of an IEP meeting might include the use of first names at the time of introduction, an aspect that is typical of the "casual intimacy" of the Anglo American communication style (Lee, 1996), which can lead to considerable confusion among many Asian (Sue & Sue, 1990), Native American (Sutton & Broken Nose, 1996), African American (Hines & Boyd-Franklin, 1996; Sue & Sue, 1990), and Mexican (Falicov, 1996) families, who are more accustomed to reserved, formal, and polite initial encounters that involve formal forms of address. In any case, because it is up to professionals to initiate these informalities, the status differential remains unaffected.

Despite legal regulations to the contrary, school districts might schedule IEP meetings according to their, not the parents', convenience (Simpson, 1996). If parents cannot attend because of conflict of time, transportation, or child care problems and are not aware of their right to participate, then they may not dispute the scheduling, choosing instead not to attend. This decision often is misperceived as an indicator that "they don't care."

Difference in status also affects interactions at meetings. Parents often are the only "outsiders," or nonprofessionals, among the participants, particularly when they are unaware that regulations allow them to bring a lawyer or a parent advocate to the meeting

(Simpson, 1996). Sometimes parents may not be introduced to the other participants, all of whom, as professional colleagues, may know each other. Whereas professionals are addressed by titles or last names, parents may be addressed by first name only (Harry, 1992c, 1992e; Marion, 1979).

These behaviors convey to parents the message that they have little or no status as members of the IEP committee. As Ware (1994) pointed out, a significant barrier to equitable collaboration among IEP committee members is the hierarchical structure of schools. Indeed, it even affects the professionals, creating a hierarchy among them that corresponds closely to the hierarchy of professional knowledge (Mehan, 1993; Mehan, Hartwick, & Meihls, 1986; Skrtic, 1995c; Ware, 1994). For instance, the psychologist enjoys the highest status, followed by the special education teacher, then the related-services professionals; the general education teacher is at the bottom of the hierarchy for professionals (Mehan, 1993). Parents, with their anecdotal and unscientific knowledge, unfortunately, rank below the general education teacher.

Often, parents are ushered into a room where all of the other participants are already present and seated, leaving the parent no choice in seating, thus amplifying the sense of being an outsider. Equally often, parents and other "temporary" members of the committee are required to leave the room while the actual decision about placement is being made (Mehan et al., 1986). As Mehan et al. (1986) asserted, this action is an unequivocal declaration of who holds power, and it denies parents influence in an area where most might be expected to hold an opinion. These attitudes are reinforced further when parents perform the ultimate "subjective" act: cry! Harry, Allen, and McLaughlin (1995) reported a meeting at which a mother who burst into tears was ushered sympathetically out of the meeting until she regained her composure. This excluded her from relevant matters that were discussed in her absence.

Because parents are cast in the role of "temporary members," their participation is defined by the professionals. If parents lack the cultural capital that would enable them to negotiate a change in this pattern of discourse, then the formal meeting becomes yet another forum for compliance with the law rather than communication in the full meaning of the term, and the absence of meaning in parent participation is startling. This is powerfully illustrated by Harry's (1992a, 1992c) description of a case in which Dora, a Puerto Rican American mother, was not even aware that a meeting that she attended was an IEP meeting. Although the event met none of the criteria for an IEP meeting, in that it was initiated by the parent, not the teacher, it took place well beyond the 30-day time limit for such meetings, and no one from the evaluation team was present, it was conducted and recorded as an IEP meeting. At the end of the meeting, the parent was handed an IEP document simply as documentation of the meeting; its nature and importance were not mentioned. As Harry noted, Dora signed the IEP

> Not knowing that an IEP was required or that there were specific procedures for its implementation . . . quite unaware of its meaning and importance in the system, and certainly unaware that the conduct of the meeting was out of compliance with state requirements. (Harry, 1992c, p. 485)

From Dora's point of view, all she had done was "talked to the teacher."

The Order of Speakers and the Types of Reporting in IEP Meetings

The hierarchy of status also becomes evident in the order in which the participants present their information about the child under consideration and the manner in which this information is presented, as studies on IEP conferences show (Bennett, 1988; Mehan, 1993). For instance, in his study, Mehan (1993) noted clearly defined parameters in keeping with the hierarchical professional structure of the school: The school psychologist presented first, followed by the child's special education teacher, the nurse, and finally the child's mother. Furthermore, the psychologist's information was presented in the form of a "single uninterrupted report" that was read aloud, "augmented by officially sanctioned props" that included the case file, test results, and prepared notes. Although the psychologist's report contained fairly technical language, such as "poor mediate recall" and "high auditory association," as well as abbreviations such as "ITPA" for the name of a test, there were no explanations for the terms used, and no questions were asked. The general education teacher's and mother's information was elicited by other members of the committee in the form of a question-and-answer session. Both spoke from memory and had no notes, and, although they used no technical terms, they were asked to clarify what they meant.

Similarly, in Bennett's (1988) study of the interactions between Hispanic parents of deaf children and special education professionals, a parent was prevented from discussing the possibility that the classroom environment was affecting her child's behavior because this knowledge did not conform to the professionals' analysis of his behavior. Thus, despite the parent's best advocacy efforts, she was effectively silenced.

Parents' silence can emerge as much from the professional imposition of the parameters for discourse as from differences in interpersonal communication styles. When the reasons for silence are not clearly understood, communication is further impeded. As an early intervention professional noted,

> I have some experience working in Appalachia. There's a way in which these people are very comfortable in being silent together. You have to put in a time of silence with them and talk in monosyllabic exchanges. It's not the kind of exchange that middle-class professionals are used to. (DeGangi et al., 1994, p. 511)

Many Native American (Sutton & Broken Nose, 1996) and Asian (Ishisaka, Nguyen, & Okimoto, 1985) families expect to have authority figures and specialists, whether they are medicine men or special education teachers, tell them what to do about their child's health and behavior problems, and they believe that the proper response to an authority figure is respectful silence. By the same token, Asian (Ho, 1987; Kim, 1996; Leung, 1988) and Native American (Red Horse, 1988) parents, who place great value on personal stoicism and containment of emotion, may prefer to remain silent rather than discuss with unknown professionals what they consider family problems. With some African American families, silence comes from a lack of trust in authority figures (Hines & Boyd-Franklin, 1996).

Differences in other aspects of interpersonal communication can also exacerbate the dissonance. Low-context communication, used by most mainstream professionals, favors a verbal approach without circumlocution, which can appear confrontational, pushy, or insensitive to those who are unfamiliar with such direct styles of communication (Lee, 1996; Simpson, 1996). Many Native American (Sutton & Broken Nose, 1996), African American (Lustig & Koester, 1993), Haitian (Bibb & Casimir, 1996), Japanese (Matsui, 1996), Indonesian (Piercy, Soekandar, & Limansubroto, 1996), Iranian (Jalali, 1996), and Mexican (Falicov, 1996) families, however, prefer high-context communication styles that provide contextual cues for listeners to understand what is being said indirectly while allowing speakers to convey respect or deference (Sutton & Broken Nose, 1996), politeness (Falicov, 1996; Piercy et al., 1996), frustration (Bibb & Casimir, 1996), disagreement (Jalali, 1996), or anger (Lee,

1996). Similarly, many Vietnamese (Leung & Boehnlein, 1996), African American (Lustig & Koester, 1993), and Puerto Rican (Garcia-Preto, 1996) families consider making direct eye contact with a speaker extremely impolite, in complete contrast to the dominant Euro-American belief (Simpson, 1996).

CONCLUSION

The authority that technical rationalism, the dominant paradigm of professional education, bestows on professional knowledge about the diagnosis and remediation of a student in special education tends to undermine parents' knowledge about their child. Furthermore, this hierarchy of knowledge and status directly contradicts the legal requirement for parent–professional collaboration in the education decision-making process, placing both parents and professionals in a precarious and unpleasant situation. To have their views considered, parents are expected to advocate vigorously—an expectation that is particularly unfair to parents who may lack an awareness of both this responsibility and the avenues for participation, such as the IEP meeting. Parents who do attend the IEP meeting then are confronted by the rigid, positivism-based hierarchical structure that belies the legal mandate. Differences in interpersonal communication style serve only to increase further the barriers to collaboration between parents and professionals.

4

Professionals' Perspectives on Parenting Styles

Maya's Story

At a dinner party at my home, I noticed my American friend's eyes grow rounder and rounder as she watched my Indian friend sit her almost 4-year-old daughter on her lap and proceed to feed her swiftly and efficiently. Later, she shook her head in amazement: "My kids learned to eat by themselves by the time they were 2! We Americans like our kids to be independent as early as possible." Then, she continued, "Speaking of kids, we need to be getting home soon. We have an early day ahead of us tomorrow. My husband is the baseball coach for our son's team, and I promised our daughter I'd watch her soccer game." Listening to her, I tried—and failed—to recall a single instance when, growing up in India, my parents played with me beyond toddlerhood. As soon as I reached an age when I understood the rules of a game and could be expected to share with peers, I played with other children. There were no parents on the sidelines cheering, keeping score, or coaching. What a high level of independence was expected of us children, I thought. It struck me that parents in all cultures seek to make children independent but that the milestones toward that goal may differ.

I remembered this incident when, some months later, I was introduced to a Native American mother, living on the reservation, who agreed to let me interview her about her adult daughter with developmental disabilities. She told me with pride that all of her adult children, many with children of their own, lived in proximity of each other on the reservation, and she beamed as she described the sundry shop that she and her husband had been able to set up in an annex of the house for their daughter with disabilities after her graduation. This way, their daughter, who was unlikely to get married or to have children of her own, could enjoy financial independence while enjoying the comforts of home. Yet another culturally defined understanding of independence, I thought.

Then I met the middle-income, Anglo American professional who had organized a parent support group on the same reservation. She described enthusiastically how she had come up with the idea and was excited that the first meeting had been fairly well attended and considered a success by all. Agreeing that it might be interesting for me to attend the next meeting and meet the mothers, she wondered in what capacity I could be introduced to them. Then she remembered that the mothers brought their children with them and that she was looking for someone who could supervise the children while the mothers attended the meeting. "Could you look after the children during the meeting?" she asked. "Do you have parenting skills?"

I realized that, like many of us professionals, she was assuming a universality of meaning to the term *parenting skills,* believing that milestones toward independence are the same and that bringing up children occurs in the same way across all cultures. Here we were, trying to use her knowledge of parenting in the Anglo American culture to assess my skills as an Indian mother and decide whether I could look after Native American children. Implicit and equally disconcerting was the unquestioning acceptance that the term conveyed an objective truth and the belief that we were demonstrating true professionalism.

When did "parenting" cease to become something that only parents and families did? When did it become acceptable, indeed, appropriate, for professionals to ask parents whether they had "parenting skills"? Some scholars might argue that the task of child rearing has always been a shared responsibility between parents and teachers, ever since going to school became part of a child's repertoire of activities (Lightfoot, 1978; Peisner, 1989). Others have noted that, over the years, the expectations for what schools teach children have changed; witness the advent of sex education, traditionally perceived as being within the realm of "parenting" (Harry & Kalyanpur, 1994).

Perhaps the timing of this blurring between what schools or professionals should do and what parents should do is less significant than its existence and most so for the field of disabilities, in which professionals target as education goals traditional parenting tasks, such as self-help and leisure skills, as much as traditional academic tasks, such as reading and writing. Indeed, it could be argued that the pendulum has swung to the point at which professionals are legally mandated to ensure that parents are involved in the child-rearing process of getting their child to learn to eat, dress, and make friends. For instance, in recommending that early education programs provide "family education and training about exemplary models and practices to the families of children in early intervention" (Turnbull & Turnbull, 1998, p. 259), Part C of the Individuals with Disabilities Education Act (IDEA) Amendments of 1997 (PL 105-17) specifically suggests that its goal is to enhance the capabilities of parents. In this climate, many people consider it perfectly appropriate for professionals to question a parent's "parenting skills" and to assume that the professionals are the experts on parenting.

Thus, with the increasing overlap between child-rearing and educational tasks, the responsibility for involving parents in the cognitive and social development of their child with disabilities has fallen on professionals. The expectation for parent participation is policy driven. Under the law, professionals are required to inform parents of any changes in their children's educational placement, of steps for an evaluation or assessment, of their rights to due process, and so forth. As described in Chapter 3, these procedures determine the legal parameters for enlisting parent involvement in the decision-making process for their child's education and can, if narrowly interpreted, inspire very rudimentary levels of parent participation.

Professional responsibility for parent participation has led to another outcome, the focus of this chapter: the enlisting of parents as "helpers" in achieving their child's education and child-rearing goals. Because the next step to identifying appropriate education goals, as documented in the individualized education program (IEP) or the individualized family service plan (IFSP), is to implement them, it is commonplace—indeed, natural—for professionals to expect parents to participate in "reinforcing" learning and helping toward "generalizability of skills across various contexts." What needs reinforcing and how is prescribed by professionals. This forms the basic premise of parent education programs and IEP goals such as, "Mary will come to school wearing socks and shoes." As we explain in this chapter, one unfortunate outcome of this interpretation of parent participation is that many professionals, in the belief that they must teach parents "parenting skills," often overlook the cultural specificity of their own professional knowledge about child rearing and development and conclude that different parenting practices are "wrong" or at least inappropriate. This has serious implications for the partnered process of identifying and implementing appropriate education goals for the child or adolescent with disabilities.

This chapter is divided into three sections. The first section examines two assumptions about parenting skills—universality and deficit—that are embedded in professional practice. The second section describes how differing social orientations, with specific reference to family values, structure, and interactions, inform "parental ethnotheories," or parents' belief systems, on child rearing (Harkness & Super, 1996). The third section examines the implications of these differing parental ethnotheories for professional practice in special education, specifically in the area of discipline and education goal setting.

ASSUMPTIONS ABOUT "PARENTING SKILLS"

Professional practice manifests two inherent assumptions about parenting skills. The first is that because child development and developmental psychology are scientifically based, the theories are objective and therefore universally applicable. Furthermore, behaviors that are considered normative by the mainstream have become the standards of behavior for all other groups. The second is that any variation from these norms is a deviation and, therefore, "wrong" practice that necessitates remediation.

Assumption of Universal Applicability

More and more, the task of child rearing no longer remains solely in the hands of parents and extended family but has come to be shared with experts and paid professionals who design, oversee, and provide services. As infants and toddlers become students and eventually young adults, they and their families encounter myriad situations in which they are presented with a value system, rules, behaviors, and expectations that may not coincide with their own. In some situations, the conflict may seem obvious, such as the IEP goal to teach an Asian child with a disability to eat with a fork and a knife when the child uses chopsticks at home (Meyers, 1992). Other instances, however, may be less overt, as in the case of the Native American parents of a young woman with developmental disabilities who found that the highly recommended self-advocacy course in which their daughter was enrolled at the local community college was making her "rebellious," whereas the professionals had recommended the course in the hope that she would become "assertive" (Kalyanpur, 1998). Similarly, M. Smith-Lewis (personal communication, February 1992) pointed to the incongruence in introducing American Sign Language, the signs and symbols for which emerge as much from English etymology as from the cultural context—for example, the sign WOMAN is a reference to bonnet strings (Livingston, 1997)—as an alternative means of communication for nonverbal children whose native language is not English.

The professionals in the examples just described are not unique in their perspective. Scientific objectivity in and of itself is considered "recommended practice" and is further fortified by theories about genetic determinism (Valsiner, 1989a), the belief that ability or disability is inherent in an individual, precluding the possible impact of externalities such as environment. This belief is embedded in traditional and dominant behaviorist and developmental paradigms, such as Piagetian theory (Valsiner, 1989a). As a result, the development of children in Western industrialized countries has come to be considered the norm for "all children of the human species" (Valsiner, 1989a, p. 1), regardless of their economic and cultural milieu. Probably the most extreme example of this oversight is the use of assessment instruments, such as the Wechsler Intelligence Scale for Children (Wechsler, 1991) and the Vineland Adaptive Behavior Scales (Sparrow, Balla, & Cicchetti, 1984), on populations that are not included in the standardized sample (Helms, 1992; Hinkle, 1994).

Assumption of Right versus Wrong Practice

As the rules, behaviors, and values of the dominant culture of Western rationalism became established as the norm within professional domains, a corollary belief arose that the values and behaviors from other cultures, not being the norm, were therefore deviant and the cultures themselves "deficit"; parents who adhered to the so-called "deviant" sets of rules were "a tangle of pathology" and their children "culturally deprived" (U.S. Department of Labor, 1965, p. 51).

Thus, not only are professionals not trained to be aware of the cultural underpinnings of their practice (Skrtic, 1995a), but they also are, in fact, trained to remediate what is perceived to be "wrong" practice. For instance, occupational therapists who develop for an Asian child an eating goal that requires the use of knife, spoon, and fork do so on the basis of two embedded assumptions: 1) that the ability to eat independently involves these and only these implements and 2) that eating with chopsticks is neither a valued nor a socially appropriate skill. Similarly, in Kalyanpur's (1998) Native American study, the child psychologist, working under the "recommended practice" mainstream assumption that children acquire language through direct and active verbal interactions with their parents (Bredekamp, 1997), identified a "language delay" in children who actually were bilingual. Because she had not observed the mothers talking to their children much and because she subscribed to the assumption of "cultural deprivation," she concluded that "the [Native American] culture was hurting them." Instances abound of African American children whose language is demeaned in school because it is not Standard English (Delpit, 1995; Heath, 1983; Piestrup, 1973), in some cases to the point that preschoolers, articulate and master storytellers at home, were placed at risk for academic failure in school (Heath, 1983; Piestrup, 1973).

This deficit model has permeated all of the helping professions. In health, social work, and mental health services, it contributes to the medical model that identifies innate deficits in children. In special education services, it contributes to the overrepresentation of culturally and linguistically diverse students in special education (see Chapter 2). In child welfare services, as we show in following sections, it provides the rationale for parent education programs and for legal safeguards against abuse and neglect by families whose parenting does not conform to the professional definition of appropriate practices.

Negative Effects of the Assumptions of Universality and Deficiency on Parent–Professional Interaction

The dual assumptions of universality and deficiency tend to affect parent–professional interactions adversely. Perhaps the best known example of this is in parent-training models, such as those devised in conjunction with compensatory education policies. Although we acknowledge that more recent approaches to parent training have attempted to respect and incorporate traditional practices among minority families, we believe that the prevailing approach has been imbued with a deficit view of minority families.

Caught between the ideal of excellence and the reality of failing students, policy makers were faced with an ineluctable choice: Either forgo excellence and a standard curriculum, or target the students who are likely to fail in school or in life and provide them with a separate curriculum (Margonis, 1992). The decision to go the latter route resulted in compensatory programs and parent education models (Laosa, 1983). The intention was that the "deficiencies" of the children and of their parents, who lacked the ability to teach their children the skills necessary for academic success, could be overcome through these compensatory and at-risk programs.

Who were these parents who needed to be taught compensatory skills? Children who were identified as being most at risk for academic failure were those whose home conditions included "poverty, low educational attainments of parents, single-parent families, and non–English-speaking families" (Levin, 1990, p. 284). As the National Commission on Children asserted,

> More and more families, overburdened and debilitated by the conditions of their lives, struggle to survive in settings where poverty, unmarried child bearing, absent fathers, unemployment, alienation, and violence are common. Under these circumstances, it is difficult for parents to teach children the value of marriage, steady work, and a healthful lifestyle. Children have few opportunities to acquire the skills, attitudes, and habits that lead to success in school, productive employment, and strong, stable families. (1991, p. xxv)

Thus, parent education programs set about the task of teaching appropriate parenting skills to "culturally disadvantaged" parents, whether poor, less educated, or linguistically diverse.

Furthermore, parenting skills deemed appropriate were those that would show parents and thereby children that "character, self-discipline, determination, and constructive service are the real substance of life" (National Commission on Children, 1991, p. xxv). Margonis noted that occupational mobility was assumed to be "the supreme educational goal" (1992, p. 348) and a value espoused by all families. Other middle-income behaviors targeted as appropriate were disciplinary practices that avoided the use of physical punitive measures (Hong & Hong, 1991).

The pernicious effect of these assumptions becomes apparent when we consider that the recognition of the cultural basis of our actions, although a difficult process for service providers, is doubly so for parents who may be struggling with the maze of special education procedures, terminology, and programs. Parent–professional discourse in special education requires a level of articulation and awareness that even middle-income parents, whose "language" may be similar to those of the professionals, find difficult to acquire (Turnbull, Turnbull, Shank, & Leal, 1999); families who do not share the same understandings are at a further disadvantage (Harry, Allen, & McLaughlin, 1995). A Korean mother of a child with disabilities described the cultural miscommunication that arose between her and a professional, Amy, on Amy's first visit to the mother's home (H. Lee, personal communication, November 20, 1996). Amy initiated some activities, and the child responded well, while the mother sat back and observed. When told later that Amy's interpretation of the situation was that the professionals would need "to make her interact more with her child," the mother commented,

> First of all, I was not sure what the purpose of the visit was. Also, in my culture, we do not show off our affection in front of strangers. However, if I had known that she wanted to see if I could interact with my child all right, I would have done it. We are very shy people and were taught not to show our emotions. Also, I was being humble and nice to Amy. I thought I could always interact with my child when professionals are not there and I would just let Amy interact with Sung-Hee for the purpose of letting Sung-Hee be exposed to diverse individuals. Amy visited my home only once. She probably had some information about my family, but I never had an informal or formal conversation with her. Was it appropriate for her to judge that my behavior indicated an inappropriate, inactive mother?

CULTURE AND PARENTAL ETHNOTHEORIES

Cross-cultural research on parenting indicates that, far from being universal, parenting styles tend to differ not only from culture to culture but also within cultural groups from family to family. Indeed, as Harkness and Super (1996) contended, "parental ethnotheories," or parent belief systems, about child rearing and development are affected by culture and personal history in ways that are unique to each family.

For many years, behaviorist and developmental paradigms dominated, spotlighting the child as an isolated unit of analysis. Later, the work of Bronfenbrenner and Vygotsky developed more dynamic, interactive models of parent–child interactions that used a broader lens to incorporate an understanding of culture into explanations of parenting. Theorists realized that much of parents' beliefs about child rearing or parental cognition are

> Not a result of reflection and acceptance or conclusion but are absorbed by the individual and are a part of the cultural and personal belief system that is so long-standing and ingrained that the individual is unaware of its existence or any alternative possibility. (McGillicuddy-De Lisi & Subramanian, 1996, p. 163)

Many writers have pointed to the transactional nature of personal beliefs and culture (Harkness & Super, 1996; McGillicuddy-De Lisi & Subramanian, 1996; Super & Harkness, 1986) whereby individuals construct personal beliefs out of their cultural knowledge and the social meanings suggested at a particular point in history, a process that Harkness and Super (1996) referred to as "instantiation." In other words, the cultural context is shared by members of a culture at particular periods in time; indeed, beliefs are appropriated directly from the culture. For instance, McGillicuddy-De Lisi and Subramanian noted that American mothers' notion of children as "active little experimenters" who must be stimulated to use their imagination, to explore, and to express themselves through play "is in every magazine, the other mothers shared this knowledge, and the supermarkets sell little gadgets to keep children safe from their own explorations, and so on" (1996, p. 164). Indeed, this view of children as active learners in the acquisition of knowledge, processing information, experimenting, and mentally organizing experiences is reflected in a range of instructional techniques that have prevailed and continue to flourish in many Western countries, from Montessori methods of teaching (Montessori, 1965) to the more recent constructivist curriculum (Drake, 1997) wherein students are expected, through a process of exploration, to construct their own meanings of phenomena.

How each individual transacts an understanding of this shared knowledge based on his or her own personal history creates a parental ethnotheory that is unique. Therefore, although parents from the same broad culture are more likely to share similar ethnotheories than parents who belong to opposite traditions—for example, Asian versus western European—there still would be individual variations depending on whether the western European parents were, say, Italian or English. For instance, in a study of Dutch, suburban American, and Tanzanian mothers' ethnotheories, Harkness and Super (1996) noted that the Dutch and American mothers had similar explanations for their 2-year-old child's tantrums—that is, a demonstration of independence—which the authors attributed to the similar traditions of Western individualism that the two groups shared. However, differences between European and American became apparent when the Dutch mothers further associated the behavior with a situational cause, such as a disruption in the child's sleep or daytime routine, whereas the American mothers associated the behavior with an aspect of their child's "strong-willed" personality. By the same token, through a more collectivist orientation, the Tanzanian mothers acknowledged differences between siblings without centering on fostering the development of individuality, instead accepting the behavior as the innate characteristics of a child at that age, and spoke of *kasinyin* (roughly translated as "that is what a child's work is").

These perspectives are significant not only because they challenge the implicit assumption of universal applicability for almost all aspects of child development and related fields, including those that might otherwise be assumed to be innately or developmentally determined (Valsiner, 1989a), but also because they indicate that members of the same culture have distinctive ethnotheories. By the same token, in the field of disabilities, parents' ethnotheories about the nature and causes of disability provide the context and structure for parents' beliefs about treatment and intervention: For instance, if parents subscribe to the cultural belief of reincarnation whereby a disabling condition is considered to be temporary because it occurs only in the individual's present life, then the family is unlikely to seek treatment or intervention for the condition (Danseco, 1997b). The following sections analyze and illustrate the impact of family values, structures, and interactions on parental ethnotheories.

The Impact of Family Values, Structures, and Interactions on Parental Ethnotheories

A considerable body of literature has sought to recognize non-Western cultural traditions or worldviews to illustrate the variations in family values, structures, and interactions that emerge from these perspectives (e.g., Lee, 1996; Lynch & Hanson, 1998; McGoldrick, Pearce, & Giordano, 1996). This research states, for instance, that the social orientation of a cultural group, whether at the micro level of a family or at the macro level of a nation, can be either "sociocentric," whereby the individual is viewed in relation to the group and any action is seen as situated within a web of interconnected relations, or "egocentric," whereby the individual is viewed as an autonomous actor in relation to the social world (Reid, 1989). This social orientation, in turn, prescribes the group's social and political organizational structure to ensure that individual members share this worldview. Thus, cultural groups with a sociocentric orientation tend to emphasize cooperation and hierarchical interdependence, are closely knit, and are likely to have extended family systems; in contrast, cultural groups with an egocentric orientation tend to focus on individualism and equality, are less cohesive, and are more likely to have nuclear families.

Although this information provides a crucial starting point at which professionals can recognize the possibility of alternative worldviews, there are some caveats in applying this "us versus them" approach to understanding individual families' values and belief systems. First, it further exacerbates a sense of distance between professionals and parents. Second, it tends to reinforce stereotypes about cultures in presenting groups as seemingly homogeneous, when, as we know, the process of understanding the social orientation and cultural values of families cannot be reduced to a formula that places them in a finite quadrant. Perhaps a better approach is to view these social orientations as being at opposing ends of a continuum along which individual families, whose parental ethnotheories are influenced as much by personal history as by culture, might range (Harry, 1997). If we recognize that myriad variables, including ethnicity or race, will have interacted to create an infinite combination of commonalities and divergences in families both from the same and across cultural groups, then the unit of analysis becomes, appropriately, the individual family.

A further step is to apply the lens of critical pragmatism and examine our epistemological assumptions in the context of these differences to avoid what Wilson-Oyelaran (1989) called an "artificial reality." If we understand that cultural values and beliefs inform family structure and interactions, which, in turn, affect parenting practices, then we might be less likely to label as "wrong" certain child-rearing practices that emerge from a family's reality (Harry, 1997). For instance, based on traditional norms of family structure (e.g., nuclear families) and individual roles (e.g., father is sole breadwinner, mother is primary caregiver), some professionals might structure home-based service provision around the mother–child dyad, a unit of analysis that has little meaning in families in which 1) there is no one designated as the primary caregiver (Hodges, Burwell, & Ortega, 1998); 2) the mother–child dyad is no more important than the father–child dyad (Turbiville, 1994), the older sibling–child dyad (Weisner, 1993), the co-wife–child dyad (Wilson-Oyelaran, 1989), or the grandmother–child dyad (Red Horse, 1988); or 3) the social context of development rarely includes any form of dyadic formation as there typically is more than one person interacting with the child at any given moment (Kalyanpur, 1996; Rao, 1996; Trawick-Smith, 1997). If the mother is unable to fulfill the responsibilities placed on her by professionals who assume that she is the sole caregiver, then it might be easy to conclude that she "does not care" or "is not involved with her child." Conversely, professionals who recognize and incorporate the alternative caregivers into service planning would be more in keeping with the family's realities (Bromwich, 1997; Trawick-Smith, 1997). An analysis of these alternative realities, with specific reference to hierarchical versus egalitarian family values, extended versus nuclear family structures, and enmeshed versus disengaged family interactions and their implications for service delivery follows.

Family Values: Equality versus Hierarchy   Families
who subscribe to the notion of equality and individualism tend to
have egalitarian family structures (Harkness & Super, 1996). For instance, as the democratic tradition in Western cultures changed to
include women, people of color, and children as having equal rights
(Friedman, 1996), previously patriarchal family structures also
changed where, in many middle-income families now, spouses
share authority and household responsibility equally (Hareven,
1982; Oughton, Wheelock, & Wiborg, 1997). In response, the field of
early childhood special education has begun to acknowledge fathers' roles in caring for a child with a disability and to recognize
the need to involve fathers equally with mothers in daily activities
as well (Turbiville, 1994). Similarly, families who emphasize equity
among siblings, whereby "the same rules apply to the child with
disabilities as to the other children" (Matuszewski, 1996, p. 192),
might prefer that the other children not take on responsibilities that
are perceived as more parental, such as caring for their sibling with
disabilities (Reid, 1989; Weisner, 1993). Studies indicate that this is
less of an issue with large Anglo American families (Gibbs, 1993)
and some Hispanic families (Harry, Rueda, & Kalyanpur, 1998)
"where the achievement expectations and caregiving responsibilities can be spread out among siblings" (Gibbs, 1993, p. 347).

Conversely, there are families who believe in a more collectivist
rather than individualistic approach, whereby family priorities and
concerns take precedence over the individual (Levy, 1996; Meyers,
1992; Zeitlin, 1996) and the need for interdependence and cooperation is of paramount significance (Wilson-Oyelaran, 1989). Such
families tend to establish a social organization that is hierarchical
with ascribed roles and status for its members, stressing duties
rather than rights (Bromwich, 1997; Kalyanpur, 1996; Wong, 1989).
Yet other families may have a collectivistic approach that emphasizes equality and individual rights (Dorris, 1989). Searching for explanations for the high incidence of fetal alcohol syndrome among
many Native American communities, for instance, Dorris (1989) asserted that the emphasis on cooperation and communality creates
opportunities for groups of people to get together and drink, while
the concomitant value placed on personal rights precludes people
from persuading others to choose not to drink even if their health is
at risk.

How might a family with these differing social orientations respond to a child with a disability, and what are the implications of
such a response for professional practice? Some Native American
(Cunningham, Cunningham, & O'Connell, 1986) and Hmong (Mey-

ers, 1992) parents of a child with disabilities may be required to inform or consult the grandparents or other concerned community elders and may have to acquiesce to their decision; although professionals may want decisions to be made quickly, they need to respect
this process and allow time for it to occur. Noting that child-
centered intervention services and individual-focused substance
abuse programs evoke low levels of participation among Native
Americans, Dorris (1989) suggested that professionals adopt a more
communal approach by appealing to a community to become responsible for the welfare of their addicted members and the good
health of their children with fetal alcohol syndrome.

Family Structures: Extended versus Nuclear   The traditional definition of a nuclear family—two parents and their children constitute a single household—has undergone a change to accommodate the many variations in family constellations, such as
single-parent, blended, adoptive or foster, and gay or lesbian families (Turnbull & Turnbull, 1997; Zinn & Eitzen, 1993). Theories on
family systems have incorporated these demographic shifts toward
developing more responsive professional practices. In all of these
various configurations, however, the spousal relationship still assumes primacy, an implicit assumption that may not apply to all
families. For example, in "kin-corporate" families (Reid, 1989), the
brother–sister relationship serves as the fundamental structuring
principle between the genders. Here, family systems may be either
matriarchal or patriarchal; same-gender siblings and their respective spouses form a large, extended family. In such families, spousal
rights are secondary to sibling rights. This traditional pattern has
been noted among African (Sudarkasa, 1981) and Native American
families (Cunningham et al., 1986). Similarly, in Maya's extended
Indian family, child-rearing decisions about a child with Down syndrome were made by the mother and her sisters, not by the mother
and her husband. Furthermore, when the child grew up, she became the responsibility of her eldest brother, a responsibility acknowledged and unquestioningly accepted by his wife because, in
this situation, the rights of the sister superseded those of the wife.

Another variable of family structure is size. In some cases, families may extend beyond the immediate nuclear group (Cross, 1995;
Hodges et al., 1998; James, 1995; Logan, 1996; Meyers, 1992; Smith,
1996) to include blood relatives, such as grandparents, aunts, and
uncles, as well as what Smith (1996) referred to as "fictive kin,"
such as godparents, community elders, and neighbors. Extended
family members may or may not reside in the same household, a
situational fluidity that may be misread as a sign of instability to

those familiar only with the nuclear family experience (Cross, 1995; Wilson-Oyelaran, 1989). For instance, among many African Americans (Bromwich, 1997), the extended family consists of a "multigenerational, interdependent kinship system" (Shimkin, Louie, & Frate, 1978, as cited in Smith, 1996, p. 33) that includes neighbors and church members in which "identified persons external to the family are treated with the same deference and respect accorded blood relatives, and the ties and obligations to the family are just as strong" (Smith, 1996, p. 33). Similarly, *padrinos*, or godparents, and *compadres*, or confidants, are examples of the adoption of nonkin among many Latino families (Hodges et al., 1998).

In separate studies of Native American families, Attneave (1982) and Red Horse (1988) provided compelling evidence of the benefits of including grandparents and elders as appropriate in the therapeutic or education decision-making process. Similarly, in Rao's (1996) study of Bengali families of children with disabilities in India, the families appealed successfully to the neighborhood children's "spirit of community and family" when inviting them to participate in play groups that included the child with a disability and when trying to stop them from teasing the child.

Overlap and fluidity of roles may also occur. In some families, in which roles and responsibilities depend on age as well as gender and an emphasis is placed on developing a sense of collective responsibility in children, older siblings often are caregivers for the younger children (Harry et al., 1998; Hines & Boyd-Franklin, 1996; Hodges et al., 1998; Reid, 1989; Tobin, Wu, & Davidson, 1989; Valsiner, 1989b; Weisner, 1993). In many migrant (Leon, 1996; Rhodes, 1996) and Black (Hines & Boyd-Franklin, 1996) families, this may be primarily for economic reasons: The parents are freed to perform subsistence tasks. Among some Samoan (Reid, 1989) and Japanese (Tobin et al., 1989) families, the goal is more social: Duty to others is inculcated from an early age. Indeed, in some Chinese, Indian (Woodson & da Costa, 1989), Yoruba (Zeitlin, 1996), and Hmong (Meyers, 1992) extended family systems, the responsibility of caring for and disciplining children often is shared among several "parent figures"—natural parents, father's other wives, aunts and uncles, grandparents, and older siblings (Wilson-Oyelaran, 1989); often, children spend as much time with alternate caregivers as with their biological mother (Hodges et al., 1998).

For families of children with disabilities, this flexibility in caregivers has implications both for informal respite and child care options and for the levels of acceptance for the member with the disability. For instance, in Harry et al.'s (1998) study, a Dominican family assumed that their son with moderate mental retardation would accompany his siblings and participate in their recreational activities. Through this responsibility, the siblings and their friends became an additional resource for playmates in an environment that was completely accepting of the boy's disabling condition. Furthermore, Harry (1998) noted that some families expect significant sibling responsibility, including child care for the sibling with disabilities, and also expect and prepare siblings for a greater role in adult responsibility for the child with the disability. Similarly, research on out-of-home placement (Borthwick-Duffy, Eyman, & White, 1987; Heller & Factor, 1991) points to greater reliance on family residence in adulthood among African American and other ethnic groups.

Family Interactions: Enmeshment versus Disengagement   Patterns of interaction between family members and with those outside the family differ from family to family; boundaries may be open or closed and establish the level of cohesion in a family. As Turnbull and Turnbull stated,

> Family cohesion refers to family members' close emotional bonding with each other as well as the level of independence they feel within the family system (Olson et al., 1980). Cohesion exists across a continuum, with high disengagement on one end and high enmeshment on the other. (1997, p. 108)

Perhaps because "most families operate in the wide swath in the center of the cohesion continuum" (Turnbull & Turnbull, 1997, p. 108), the blurring of roles and boundaries that occurs among highly enmeshed families often is interpreted as being negative and indicative of chaotic family interactions rather than as a strength (Simon, 1996). For instance, as Hines and Boyd-Franklin (1996) pointed out, the perception that many African American families consist of "female-headed households" actually is an adaptive response to role reversal among husbands and wives who are faced with low employment for males. Similarly, the practice of informal adoption or "child keeping" in times of economic necessity among extended family members in the African American community (Hines & Boyd-Franklin, 1996) means that children and other relatives may have lived with different families at different times; emotional bonds in these cases may have little connection with physical proximity or bloodline.

Studies on the issue of privacy and space in interpersonal communication styles also reveal differences across cultures (Hall, 1983; Lustig & Koester, 1993). For instance, a Guyanan father was highly distressed when his preschool son with autism, who would fall to the ground to indicate that he did not want to be touched, was taught to push his classmates away instead. While the professionals believed that they were teaching the boy a survival skill toward assertiveness, the father saw the learned behavior as extremely rude and very socially inappropriate.

Strongly enmeshed families that prefer to resolve problems within the boundaries of the family or, at the most, the extended family would view the professional as an outsider. Such families might resent the professional's insistence on being included in the problem solving. For instance, in Rao's (1996) study, the Bengali mothers believed that when family problems were discussed with an outsider, the cohesion of the family was threatened. When professionals operate from the deficit model, this interaction may be misperceived. In Kalyanpur's (1998) Native American study, the mothers on the reservation interpreted their phrase, "We look after our own," as an indication of the close and caring nature of their culture, whereas the professionals translated it in terms of a closed, even hostile community. By the same token, professionals who respond to families from a strengths-based perspective are less likely to be viewed as outsiders (Bibb & Casimir, 1996; McKenzie-Pollock, 1996).

Research indicates that the intercommunicative structure and group-dynamic expectations of the support group, a popular and common mainstream strategy for uniting individuals with a common issue and addressing parents' emotional and educational needs, often is antithetical to patterns of interactions in some families. For instance, in their study of a Latino support group for parents of children with developmental disabilities, Shapiro and Simonsen (1994) found that the tradition of *confianza,* or trust, initially made many participants reluctant to share their experiences in the "instant intimacy" environment of the support group. Similarly, in a study of Latino families, Lieberman (1990) noted that the mothers sought opportunities to be alone with the group coordinator rather than attend the group meetings, preferring the privacy and closeness of the individual sessions to discuss freely the same personal and child-rearing issues scheduled for discussion at the group sessions.

Group Status and Community Identity

Some families perceive status to be a shared commodity whereby social transgressions by an individual have shameful consequences for the entire family or community. In these circumstances, idiosyncratic or individualistic behavior rarely is tolerated, and, instead, a high value is placed on conformity. Thus, the stigma of deviance or disability affects not only the individual and his or her immediate family but also the group associated with this family. As Harry's (1992a, 1992d) study of Puerto Rican families demonstrated, the professional labeling of an individual child as "retarded" was devastating to the families because it implied that the entire community was at fault. Similarly, Ballenger (1994) noted that disciplinary practices among the Haitian families whose preschool children she taught made the children accountable to the entire community: They were told that if they behaved badly, then they would make their parents, aunts, and uncles "sad."

Furthermore, individual status is relational and dependent on one's position in society. In many Native American (Red Horse, 1988; Sutton & Broken Nose, 1996) and Asian (Kao & Lam, 1997) families, for instance, elders and young children are accorded high status. Certain families may have higher status within a community than others (Lee, 1996; Meyers, 1992). Under the hierarchical structure, status may also be gender specific or according to birth order, such as the firstborn son's having higher status than his younger brothers and both older and younger sisters. By contrast, in the mainstream culture, in which the ideal of equality generates social mobility, individuals acquire status through their own identity or occupation, such as a profession or a successful business (Oughton et al., 1997). Because parameters of status are an aspect of "invisible culture" that becomes apparent with sustained contact (Philips, 1983), professionals who, in initial interactions, impose inappropriate understandings of status when working with parents may show disrespect when none was intended. For instance, the mainstream service providers in Kalyanpur's (1998) study of a Native American parent support group accorded a high status to the Native American professionals and a lesser status to the participants, although the latter group included members of the two highly respected families on the reservation, thus quite unwittingly alienating themselves from the Native American mothers.

In studies on community and social networks, researchers have identified socioeconomic status (SES) as a major variable in the types of supports that individuals developed (see Traustadottir, 1995, for a review). Members of middle SES tended to develop networks and friendships based on such commonalities as occupation/ profession or recreational interests, whereas working-class families sought kin- and neighborhood-based communities and friendships. Other factors also may contribute to a sense of community. Although in some cases African Americans tend to divide along socioeconomic lines, the common experience of racism and being Black also can facilitate a sense of a larger community across all classes as well as among "voluntary immigrants" (Ogbu, 1987) from Africa and the Caribbean (Logan, 1996; Ogbu, 1987). Similarly, as Harry pointed out, although the racial, national, and socioeconomic heterogeneity of Latinos makes generalizations about this group difficult, the Spanish language, despite many prevailing dialects, is a single common bond that "seems to stand as an important symbol of their cultural heritage and solidarity" (1992a, p. 25). Among Asians, communities are more tightly drawn along country of origin; families tend to migrate and settle in pockets that are already occupied by their fellow compatriots, historically for economic reasons, as in the case of Chinese railroad and laundry workers in San Francisco (Burger, 1977) or the Indian Sikh farmers in California (Gibson, 1987) and, more recent, through government intervention, as in the case of the Hmong (Fadiman, 1997; Trueba, Jacobs, & Kirton, 1990). Furthermore, certain commonalities, such as history (Meyers, 1992), ethnicity (Lee, 1996), and religion, can help create a common context among groups. Geographic isolation on reservations, as occurs with many Native American communities (Arden, 1987), in ghettos such as Harlem (Logan, 1996) and Chinatown (Burger, 1977), or in certain neighborhoods such as within inner cities, further enhances group identity.

The impact of these variables as contributory factors to group identity often is overlooked. For instance, for many non–native-English-speaking parents whose child with a disability may have difficulty acquiring language, the decision to forgo teaching the child the native tongue in favor of English, the language preferred in the mainstream, may be akin to the loss of connection with one's cultural heritage; as an Indian mother noted, the "major, immediate impact" in switching from Hindi to English to communicate with their daughter with a hearing impairment was accepting that they "would raise a child not rooted in Indian values" (Das, 1995, p. 6). Similarly, in Harry's (1992b, 1992d) study, the geographical differences in the boundaries of the Puerto Rican community and those of the school district had the parents alarmed that their children were being sent to schools "so far away" from the Hispanic neighborhood in which they lived.

We have seen the impact of family values, structures, and interactions on parental ethnotheories on child rearing and the implications for professional practice. For instance, families that adhere to a sociocentric orientation of cooperation and collectivism are unlikely to raise children who are mindful of their rights to self-determination. Expecting these parents to want their child with disabilities to make personal choices and acquire personal autonomy without an adequate understanding of their parental ethnotheory may alienate the family. Similarly, families with large, extended family systems are more likely to raise children among multiple caregivers and would be better served in home-based services that involve these alternative resources for parenting. Again, strongly enmeshed families are more likely to perceive professionals as outsiders; yet group affiliations may create an element of bonding that is not immediately apparent to outsiders. The next sections examine areas in which professional expectation for parent involvement is highest and, if intersected by differing ethnotheories, also the most conflicted: discipline and education goals.

PARENTING AND DISCIPLINARY PRACTICES

So far, our analysis has focused on the values that parents might inculcate in their children and the ways in which certain variables, such as family structure, might determine which values a family would deem appropriate. Now we examine the process by which this inculcation of values, or the process of socialization, occurs. More specific, we analyze the factors that affect parents' decisions about the process—that is, why parents choose certain parenting and disciplinary practices over others to socialize their child. We identify some of the ideological and societal changes that have taken place in the United States and that have contributed to a shift in beliefs from an authoritarian to a democratic mode. We describe how this change in focus affects families who have adopted this canon.

Authoritarian versus Democratic Parenting Practices

Adults are responsible for facilitating children's acquisition of appropriate behaviors through a process of socialization. This process can involve explicitly teaching children the rules for behavior—in other words, disciplining them. The specific disciplinary practices in which parents engage emerge from their general beliefs about child rearing that, in turn, are influenced by the information that they read on the subject, by people whom they seek for advice, and by their own experiences both as a child and as a parent (Peisner, 1989). For example, Matuszewski, an Anglo American mother, used similar strategies to develop parenting skills for her son with disabilities:

> My [parenting] techniques were a blend, modeled after those of my
> mother, grandmother, aunt, and newly acquired friends who brought

techniques from their own families with them. . . . I accepted the professionals' recommendations to read everything they presented to me. I
gathered pamphlets and booklets and kept them by the bedside. I took
the dusty parenting books off the shelves and opened them up one
more time, and I went to "support" group meetings to meet other parents "just like" me. (1996, p. 191)

What follows is an analysis of the religious, sociological, and
epistemological traditions that have affected the ethnotheories
about discipline that parents over the years may have acquired.
Many child-rearing and disciplinary practices in 19th- and 20th-
century America can be traced back to three different traditions:
1) ancient Hebrew, Greek, and Roman practices; 2) Puritan beliefs;
and 3) Locke's and Rousseau's ideas of the rational child (Peisner,
1989). The impact of industrialization and urbanization on family
life, however, produced a transactional change in the cultural
philosophies about child rearing to create a worldview that is
uniquely American. These developments are briefly summarized
next (for a fuller analysis, see Butchart, 1998).

Religious Influences   The religious tradition that has influenced disciplinary practices in the United States most significantly is the Judeo-Christian ethic that originated in the Hebrew,
Greek, and Roman traditions. In these traditions, parenting styles
primarily were authoritarian. All three civilizations agreed about
the necessity for discipline and control, both at home and in school.
Children were seen as unformed and moldable, with tendencies toward disorder if left unguided but also valued as the future of the
family and society. Initially, parents were responsible for bringing
up their children to be moral citizens; children, in turn, were expected to show unquestioning obedience. Later, the role of parents
as educators was taken over by professional teachers. Corporal punishment was clearly emphasized; children received spankings,
beatings, and whippings in the course of their education. Although
Puritan conceptions of the child varied in that children were seen
as entering the world imbued with original sin and needing both instruction and strict discipline from their parents to ensure their
moral salvation, disciplinary practices stayed much the same: To
shame a recalcitrant child, parents could admonish, beat, whip, or
spank.

The aspects of Judeo-Christian traditions of disciplining that
were incorporated into American philosophies of childhood included the emphasis on parents' responsibility for children's proper
moral development and the need for establishing parental authority
and strict obedience through corporal punishment. Thus, parenting

styles were authoritarian, and physical disciplining was widely accepted. Indeed, given the aversion in the 1990s to corporal punishment among many parents and professionals, the recentness of mainstream rejection of this disciplinary practice is remarkable.

Sociological Influences In the early 1900s, the advent of Western rationalist thought encouraged parents to appeal to the rational side of children in their discipline. Philosophers such as Locke and Rousseau believed that punishment would merely teach children to avoid externally caused pain rather than to develop rational self-control that would lead to a productive life. The concept of self-discipline or taking moral responsibility for one's own behavior and of raising children to work to their full capacity became guiding themes of the Protestant work ethic, as well as enduring American ideals. The concomitant rise of the new ideals of independence, individualism, and self-sufficiency engendered by free-market economics led to an erosion of authoritarian and patriarchal structures (Friedman, 1996). These ideals first were seen in the emancipation of slaves, then the women's suffrage movement in the 1920s, the civil rights movement (the coattails of which the disability rights movement clung to) in the 1950s, and finally the culmination of the children's rights perspective in the 1970s. The last movement, spearheaded by the International Labor Organization in an effort to repeal child labor practices, encapsulated a paradigmatic role shift for all children from member of the labor force to student, endowed with rights.

Epistemological Influences Since the mid-1940s, ideas about child rearing have changed dramatically as professional beliefs about disciplinary practices have been influenced by the newly developing fields of child and behavioral psychology. Under the guise of scientific objectivity, the rational authoritarianism of medical experts began to replace parental authority, the view of "mother knows best" changed to "experts know best" (Peisner, 1989, p. 133), and the ethnotheories of many parents, mostly Caucasian middle income (Hong & Hong, 1991), were instantiated in these new directions.

The tenet in child psychology that probably has contributed most to theories about discipline is the importance of continuity in children's development. The assumption is that continuity in the socialization practices of various caregivers is beneficial to children's social and emotional development, whereas discontinuity may result in less than optimal development (Butchart, 1998). Children must infer general rules for behaving from specific disciplinary experiences. Consistent socialization messages facilitate a child's learning these rules.

Behavioral psychologists perceive discipline as one type of social learning that leads to an increase or a decrease in the frequency of some behavior according to its consequences. These consequences can be positive (i.e., rewarding) or negative (i.e., punitive) in nature. Desirable behaviors are rewarded to encourage their maintenance, whereas undesirable behaviors are punished through the contingent use of aversive verbal, physical, or psychological techniques, such as scolding, spanking, isolation, or withdrawal of privileges.

Although these basic tenets of behavioral psychology remain essentially unchanged, modifications have allowed that thoughts and emotions have an impact on the child's reactions (Beyer, 1998). For instance, child psychologists noted that if a child did not think of a particular action or object as desirable, then the object would not be effective as a reward to reinforce certain behaviors. Similarly, a child who gets noticed only for inappropriate behavior may actually perceive the punishment as a reward. In other words, the intentions of a reward or a punishment may be defined by the disciplinary agent, but its effects are determined by the child.

This new understanding contributed to the relatively recent mainstream movement away from the use of corporal punishment as an appropriate disciplinary practice to using verbal, redirective approaches (Butchart, 1998). A process of instantiation then occurred within this cultural context: As professional beliefs about disciplinary practices changed, so, too, did the beliefs of those middle-income, mainstream parents who were most likely to seek professional advice and to be influenced by reading information on the subject. Parents who did not subscribe to the practices that fell within the parameters that are outlined in this section became the target of parent education programs, and many were labeled "abusive." The next section illustrates this process.

Cultural Parameters of Child Abuse versus Acceptable Discipline

The shift from corporal punishment to verbal, redirective discipline has been adopted so universally among most professionals and many Anglo American middle-income parents (Hong & Hong, 1991) as the current canon or "recommended practice" that legal safeguards against what are perceived to be "inappropriate practices" have been established (Howing & Wodarski, 1992; Janek, 1992; Mahoney, 1995). Indeed, in their zeal to proselytize parents to the good cause of verbal redirection, many professionals forget how recent the conversion of their own field has been and are apt to perceive parents whose parenting styles fall outside these norms of accept-able discipline as inadequate. An analysis of two issues—spanking and healing practices—surrounding this controversy follows.

Spanking Perhaps on no other topic has the difference in per-spectives on "acceptable disciplining" generated more controversy than the issue of spanking, as studies on mothers' disciplinary prac-tices and attitudes toward child maltreatment show (Buriel, Mer-cado, Rodriguez, & Chavez, 1991; Hong & Hong, 1991; Janko, 1994; Kalyanpur & Rao, 1991). For instance, Janko (1994) indicated that al-though many middle-income, Anglo American families engage in democratic, dialogic disciplining styles, there are many Anglo American families who do not—in particular, those of low socioeco-nomic status. Indeed, this latter group constitutes the majority of parents who are reported to child protection services for being "abu-sive." The African American mothers in Kalyanpur and Rao's (1991) study indicated that a difference in disciplining styles was a major source of distrust and dissonance in their relationships with profes-sionals. To the women, good parenting meant inculcating a sense of responsibility in the children by being strict with them; spanking was their last resort to discipline their children. What is significant is that they took great pains to distinguish between "beating up" and "spanking," the former being perceived as an abusive form of pun-ishment, a distinction that, the mothers pointed out, the profession-als did not make.

Similarly, both the foreign- and native-born Mexican American mothers in a study by Buriel et al. (1991) used spankings, although less often than scolding or deprivation of privileges. The spankings were always accompanied by an explanation; the combination of spanking with verbal reasoning possibly represented a "culturally unique disciplinary style" (Buriel et al., 1991, p. 91). Again, Chinese immigrants in Hong and Hong's (1991) study, when asked to rate their responses to vignettes involving child mistreatment, were less critical of the use of physical force by parents than were Hispanics and Caucasians. Furthermore, the Chinese and the Mexican Ameri-can mothers in the Buriel et al. (1991) and the Hong and Hong (1991) studies were reticent about recommending agency intervention in cases in which the child's welfare was not threatened. The authors attributed this finding to the cultural value of "familism" that is common to both groups, or the belief that the family is primarily re-sponsible for the welfare of its members, and issues such as how children are reared are internal matters. It is significant that al-though all of these families amply demonstrated their ability to be responsible parents and used spanking as one kind of disciplining practice, usually as a last resort, the very fact that they did made them potential targets for being reported to child welfare services as being abusive.

Healing and Medical Practices   What is a common healing or medical practice in one family might be considered unacceptable or even abusive in another. Some cultures perform circumcision on male infants; other cultures would consider the practice abusive. In some Pacific Islander families, crying infants are quieted by gentle rubbing of their genitals (Cross, 1995), a practice that would constitute sexual abuse in the United States.

Forjuoh (1995) noted that traditional healing practices among some Ashanti families of Ghana might entail intentionally inflicting burns by flame or contact with a hot object to cure childhood convulsions and seizure disorders. However, the bruises that result from these practices are indicators of abuse by mainstream American standards (Howing & Wodarski, 1992; Mahoney, 1995). The practice of *cao gio,* whereby a warmed coin is rubbed briskly over an ailing child's body until redness occurs, is a common folk remedy among some Chinese (Hong & Hong, 1991), Hmong (Fadiman, 1997), and Vietnamese (Gray & Cosgrove, 1985) families. Hong and Hong (1991) cited the case of a Vietnamese father who was arrested and jailed for alleged child abuse because he administered *cao gio* to his son. To the authorities, the marks on the child had only one "right" explanation. However, coming from a culture in which parental authority is held in high esteem, the father could not tolerate the stigma and humiliation of the accusation and subsequently committed suicide.

Once again, in all of these cases, there is no malice, no intent to harm the child. On the contrary, these most extreme measures are attempts at healing by parents and caregivers who care intensely about the welfare of their child. And yet, once again, the very fact of engaging in an "unacceptable practice" makes parents vulnerable to intervention from child welfare services. We are not implying that we advocate a kind of laissez-faire attitude of "anything goes." As professionals, we do not need to accept the situation, but by understanding the rationale behind the practice, we may use it as a springboard from which to present families with alternatives, couching them in terms that are meaningful to the families. To attribute neglect or abuse and remove a child from his or her present conditions would hardly endear any intervening professionals to a family. If, however, we explicitly acknowledge the parents' efforts and point out that providing their child with medical care can be an extension of these efforts that would eventually benefit both them and the child, then the family would be more likely to respond favorably.

Parenting Styles and the Child Welfare System

The extraordinarily narrow lens of child welfare systems cannot and does not see beyond the "brute fact" of a bruise to allow the possibility of alternative realities that might explain its existence. Although this shortsightedness may be absurd in some situations—as, for instance, when the "Mongolian spots" that appear on many children of color are mistakenly thought to be bruises and signs of abuse (Cross, 1995)—in other situations, as in the case of the Vietnamese father cited previously (Hong & Hong, 1991), the consequences may be infinitely more serious. To suggest that parents are inadequate when they are bringing up their children as they best know how is, at the very least, an injustice to them.

First, applying this narrow lens neglects to consider the possibility of alternative parenting styles that are appropriate to the family or the environment in which the child is being reared. For instance, an African American grandmother, mindful of the violence that surrounded her grandchildren who were growing up in an inner city, had taught them to "move away" from the scene of the crime:

> If you see a body laying on the street and you see people crying around it, you don't go there and touch that body, try to help. Because just as you do that, the police walk up on you with your hands on it, you did it. When you could have went the other way. You know, not running away from trouble, but avoiding it if you see it coming, you go the other way. You ain't got to go to it. (Danseco, 1997a, p. 96)

This parenting style starkly contrasts with the style of a Jewish American professional mother who taught her children to "become involved in the community and always help if you see someone in trouble" (S. Sonnenschein, personal communication, July 14, 1997). In both cases, the parenting styles matched the requirements of the environment in providing the children with the skills to survive and become competent adults.

Second, it assumes that appropriate parenting can be taught through parent education programs. As a result, numerous programs have been developed to teach parents how to parent in the hope that increased parenting abilities will result in decreased incidence of child abuse and neglect (Cameron & Vanderwoerd, 1997). Despite the prophylactic appearance of these models, however, the parents who are adjudicated to undergo this training are not new or prospective parents who might indeed benefit from some helpful tips on parenting but families who, lacking economic resources and social supports, have struggled over a period of time to maintain a fragile equilibrium before collapsing. Indeed, as Janko (1994) pointed out, the crisis-oriented approach of the child welfare system and its inability to interpret crisis as more of a process than a discrete event preempts a preventive stance whereby families could be helped through economic assistance and other supports before a crisis occurs. She cited the case of an Anglo American, low-income mother who learned quickly that the only way to trigger an avalanche of help from social services agencies was to admit voluntarily to abuse on a periodic basis, a strategy that she used quite effectively a number of times.

Over the years, the shift in professional thinking about disciplinary practices in the United States, from an authoritarian style that allowed the use of corporal punishment to a democratic mode that emphasizes verbal redirection and other alternatives to physical disciplining, has contributed to changes in parental ethnotheories about child rearing among many middle-income, Anglo American families as well. Conversely, many families' ethnotheories do not conform to this new paradigm. Because the ethnotheories emerge from families' alternative realities, or the social and philosophical factors that have an impact on their lives, families' child-rearing strategies are perfectly adequate for helping their children grow into competent adults within their specific environments. The deficit model of parent–professional interaction, however, either overlooks these alternative realities altogether or fails to account for their cultural appropriateness; as a result, many of these families are labeled "bad" or "abusive." In the next section, we examine yet another area that can be a potential source of conflict in parent–professional interactions: educational expectations and goal setting.

GOAL SETTING FOR STUDENTS: PARENTS' VERSUS PROFESSIONALS' EXPECTATIONS

When the responsibility of targeting instruction to meet certain education and socialization goals is shared among parents and extended family on the one hand and experts and paid professionals on the other—parties who may or may not hold similar child-rearing beliefs and values—examining the assumptions underlying those very goals is important. Much of special education practice is based on the assumption that children's developmental milestones are biologically determined—a yardstick that ensures scientific objectivity and therefore universal applicability. Thus, most adaptive behavior scales are developed on the understanding that children acquire mastery over specific tasks at particular ages (Hinkle, 1994).

Increasingly, however, cross-cultural research points to the cultural specificity of developmental expectations or timetables. Comparisons of mothers' timetables across cultural communities found variations in acquisition of skills as "biologically predetermined" as infant crawling and toilet training as well as those more socially defined such as verbal communication (deVries & deVries, 1977; Edwards, Gandini, & Giovaninni, 1996; Levy, 1996; McGillicuddy-De Lisi & Subramanian, 1996). Indeed, developmental expectations (i.e., education and socialization goals) emerge from the culture into which children are being socialized to become competent and responsible adults; those deemed most appropriate and significant by the adults in that culture are most likely to be the focus of the socialization process. As Edwards et al. stated,

> Timetables relate to the boundaries, or zones, for acceptable behavior that adults draw around their internalized norms for child development; they measure what adults consider to be normal in the way of earliness or lateness for particular child competencies to appear. . . . As Spindler (1987) put it, child development is susceptible to "cultural compression"; high expectations on the part of adults for mature behavior may translate into early and strong demands for mature behavior in that domain. (1996, p. 271)

Furthermore, although certain tasks, such as getting dressed or communicating with others, may appear universal, the goals that are embedded in a specific task might differ. For instance, although most cultures focus on verbal skill acquisition as a desirable goal for their children, the Anglo American families in Edwards et al.'s (1996) study wanted their children to become verbally assertive and to state their own needs, the Nepali families in Levy's study expected their children to develop moral reasoning and to be "discursively thoughtful to make internal or external logical arguments" (1996, p. 139), and the Tanzanian mothers in McGillicuddy-De Lisi and Subramanian's (1996) study hoped that their children would learn obedience and responsibility. In each case, the rationalizations emerged from the parental ethnotheories and social orientation of each family: These Anglo American families valued individuality and independence (Edwards et al., 1996), the Nepali reflected their Hindu orientation that self is constituted from membership in society (Levy, 1996), and the Tanzanian mothers brought a collectivist perspective of society to their child rearing (McGillicuddy-De Lisi & Subramanian, 1996).

Because of the uniqueness of parental ethnotheories, rationalizations can differ from family to family. For instance, in a study of American mothers, Kindermann and Valsiner (1989) noted that the mothers identified several different goals that were embedded in the single task of getting a child dressed, ranging from the immediate goal of keeping the child warm or socially appropriate (adjusted to the cultural norms of body exposure in different social environments) to guiding the child to social goals of interaction and cooperation. To describe all of the variations in maturational milestones that might occur both across and within cultures is beyond the scope of this chapter (for a review, see Edwards et al., 1996). For our purposes, we focus on three that have become cornerstone goals in special education practice: independence, individuality, and work.

Independence

As this chapter's opening story illustrated, parents in all cultures seek to make their children independent, competent adults in their respective societies. However, the meaning of independence as well as the milestones or transition markers might differ from family to family.

Differences in the Meaning of Independence   The contemporary term for independence is *self-competence,* a multidimensional construct that seeks to develop self-esteem, self-determination, and effective coping in children and adolescents with disabilities by enhancing their perceptions of personal efficacy and worthiness (Powers, Singer, & Sowers, 1996). Perceptions of worthiness and efficacy are acquired through positive attachments to caregivers, friendships, and opportunities for expressions of increasing levels of independence and autonomy; self-esteem is grounded in these perceptions. *Self-determination* is the ability to decide and act on one's own behalf; *coping* refers to individual responses to manage stressful situations.

Most significant to our argument about differences in the meaning of *independence* is the emphasis in all of these constructs on the individual. Although the definitions do acknowledge relationships with caregivers and friends, the embedded assumption is of an egocentric social orientation whereby the ultimate goal is to make the individual with disabilities totally self-reliant (Renz-Beaulaurier, 1998). For instance, as Renz-Beaulaurier pointed out, the entire focus of the field of medical rehabilitation has been on "restoring patients to the fullest levels of physical functioning" (1998, p. 75), thereby minimizing their dependence on other people.

This dedication to self-competence may appear singularly misplaced to families for whom the sociocentric alternative of interdependence is perfectly viable (Meyers, 1992; Miles, 1997; Shwalb, Shwalb, & Shoji, 1996). First, in such families, members can be independent and have distinct identities without expecting autonomy. Second, being dependent is not necessarily a devalued position; indeed, members are expected to turn to each other for help and to provide that help (Meyers, 1992). For instance, in their study, Shwalb and his colleagues (1996) were surprised to note that Japanese mothers consistently identified dependence, or *amaembo,* as a desirable personality trait in their children. They realized that the concept meant "spoiled child" to them as Western researchers but connoted reliance to the mothers who, when asked to describe illustrative behaviors, gave examples such as asking for a hug and for help with toileting, eating, or dressing.

Differences in the Milestones Toward Independence
Checklists of developmental milestones as measures of children's growth become inadequate when the milestones themselves differ from family to family. For instance, Joe (1997) noted that many Navajo mothers are more likely to be able to remember their child's first laugh rather than his or her first words or steps. Similarly, Mallory (1995) distinguished between developmental transitions (e.g., puberty) and institutional transitions (e.g., graduating from high school) and noted that the rarity of the two coinciding has implications for social policy. Differing perceptions of transitions to adulthood can have especially significant implications for services for young adults.

Independence in Adulthood
Attaining identity as an adult is a crucial aspect of the transition to adulthood. The symbolic construction of an adult identity often is marked by rites of passage that may vary among families. In some families, the transition may be biologically determined through onset of puberty and signified, for instance, through ceremonies that mark the onset of menstruation in a young girl. In other families, the marker may be chronologically based and be signified in coming-of-age parties and debuts at the age of 16 or 18. Although in some cases this developmental transition may be sufficient to acquire identity as an adult, in others, the institutional transition of marriage may be the more widely acknowledged rite of passage to adulthood.

In other families, achieving adult status may involve another central aspect: the practical setting up of a household (Magnussen, 1997). The understanding is that when individuals acquire financial independence, they will set up a physically separate establishment; where gender equality is valued, expectations will be similar for both sons and daughters. Indeed, the two dominant themes of transition services, as defined in federal policy, are gainful, competitive employment and emancipation from the family home (Mallory, 1995; Shafer & Rangasamy, 1995).

Analyzing the role of social policy in life-cycle transitions, Mallory (1995) asserted that policies have been more responsive to institutional transitions than to developmental transitions. He cited the issue of guardianship, whereby the age of majority is defined in state laws as 18 regardless of whether young adults with disabilities have indeed acquired the levels of maturity and competence needed to make independent decisions, as an example of institutional transition that may not reflect "the complex issues of time, individual and family transitions, and sociocultural context" (Mallory, 1995, p. 218). This discrepancy might affect both mainstream and diverse families.

Furthermore, Shafer and Rangasamy (1995) pointed out that the two themes of transition services are based on the values of an urban, Anglo culture and may not be compatible with the values of other groups. In their study of transition services for White Mountain Apache youth residing on reservations and maintaining traditional tribal customs, they found that "the values of cooperation, interdependence, and communal responsibility and action often conflict with the values of independence and competition that are implied by transition services" (Shafer & Rangasamy, 1995, p. 61) and questioned the validity of the policy-driven focus on the movement from the parental or natural home to other living arrangements. More than 75% of both general and special education Apache students who exited the school system continued to live with their parents, and 25% of both groups indicated that they were not interested in leaving their family home.

Indeed, among many families, it is assumed that the son will continue to live in the parents' home, regardless of economic or marital status, and that the daughter will leave after marriage only to move in with her husband's family (Harry & Kalyanpur, 1994; Harry et al., 1998; Turnbull & Turnbull, 1996). In Turnbull and Turnbull's study, for instance, the Latin American parents viewed the possibility of their unmarried children moving out of their home and establishing homes of their own upon attaining majority as "a tragedy" and "a shame on the family" (1996, p. 200).

Differences in families' orientation toward time also have implications for planning for transition. Whereas some families may prefer not to look too far ahead (Locust, 1988; Turnbull & Turnbull, 1996), others may not have such an option (Zeitlin, 1996). For instance, the Latin American families in Turnbull and Turnbull's study generally tended not to "think about the future" but to "take life a day at a time" (1996, p. 200), attributing this tendency to the value placed on interdependence. This contrasts with the expectations of some migrant (Hunter, 1982; Leon, 1996; Pyecha & Ward, 1982) and Yoruba (Zeitlin, 1996) families, whose children are forced into early independence for economic reasons.

All families aspire to make their children independent, but the markers for and meanings of independence may differ. Some families seek an interdependence whereby dependence is not a devalued position, all members depend on each other for help, and identities are distinct without being autonomous. Differences in the milestones toward independence suggest potential conflict in education goal setting, particularly in the context of social policies that tend to focus more on institutional rather than developmental transitions.

Individuality

The ideal of self-competence includes independence not only on a practical level, whereby individuals with disabilities rely minimally on others in performing everyday activities, but also on a philosophical level, whereby people can take control of their lives through the power of choice, a process that is referred to as *self-determination.* The concept of self-determination has its ideological roots in disability rights movements, which have focused on the rights of individuals with disabilities to be integrated and have equality of opportunity (Ward, 1996). In this section, we examine aspects of self-determination in which there is potential for conflict in education goal setting: the expectation that children are individuals with rights to maximizing their potential and the ideal of personal choice.

The Child as an Individual with Rights to Maximize His or Her Potential   The idea that children have the right to maximize their potential is embedded in the philosophy of self-determination and emerges from the mainstream-value emphasis on individualism. There are two values that are implicit in this premise: 1) that children are individuals and have rights and 2) that children, as individuals with rights, should be given opportunities to maximize their potential. That arguments for changes in services and attitudes toward people with disabilities in the United States have been made on the platform of individual rights and equality is no coincidence: These values are part of the collective conscience (Friedman, 1996; Powers, Singer, & Sowers, 1996; Renz-Beaulaurier, 1998; Ward, 1996). It also is not a coincidence that these same values are an integral part of educational programming, as self-advocacy courses, for adolescents and adults with disabilities to en-

able them "to speak for yourself, to make decisions for yourself, to know what your rights are, and to 'stick up' for yourself when your rights are being violated or diminished" (Lehr & Taylor, 1986, p. 3).

The egocentric orientation of such an approach focuses on the individual and assumes that all individuals, including children, have certain inalienable rights. This might be counter to the approach that a family with a more sociocentric orientation might adopt. Families who define *self* in terms of other people through a web of reciprocal relationships whereby an individual's identity is connected to his or her social identity (Wong, 1989) may neither emphasize autonomy or self-determination nor believe that depriving individuals of the opportunity to acquire such a self-concept is a violation of their rights. Such parents may not want to have their adult child with disabilities attend self-advocacy courses (Kalyanpur, 1998).

The other assumption that is embedded in the idea of individual rights is that every individual has the right to maximize his or her potential. This is one of the premises on which the principle of normalization (Wolfensberger, 1972) is based: providing opportunities to encounter the normal developmental experiences of the life cycle so that individuals with disabilities can learn about their abilities and potential and build their self-esteem (Ward, 1996). The ideal of maximization of potential is tied to the American values of occupational mobility, whereby people are responsible for constructing themselves as individuals in a multitude of alternative ways (Magnussen, 1997; Margonis, 1992), as well as of freedom of choice, whereby people make active choices about who they want to be and how they want to live (Magnussen, 1997).

Valsiner noted, however, that the maximizing orientation may be antithetical to families who subscribe instead to what he called a "satisficing perspective" (1989b, p. 74). Instead of linear, upward progression, success is measured in concentric, ever-broadening circles as individuals aspire to be the best at what they are; thus, a cobbler's son does not aspire to become a schoolmaster, which in his ascribed role as cobbler he cannot, but the best cobbler within the largest circle of community possible (Chung, 1992b; Kalyanpur & Harry, 1997; Valsiner, 1989b). This perspective ties in to a belief in hierarchical interdependence, whereby people with disabilities are not stigmatized because they are dependent because, in a way, everybody is dependent on each other and everybody has a social role, no matter what one's status is (Kalyanpur & Harry, 1997). It also ties in to a belief in value inequality (Miles, 1981), whereby people are not equal and only groups, not individuals, can be socially mobile, if at all. For instance, in Gwaltney's (1970) study of a village in Central America, he noted that the predetermined occupation for elderly blind men was begging. Mehta (1972) wrote about rural India, where young boys with developmental disabilities are expected to look after the cows. Haq (1970) stated that in the Middle East, men with visual impairments traditionally either become musicians or join the clergy. Locust (1988) told the story of Bear, the boy with developmental disabilities who was in harmony with his environment as the water carrier for his Native American village.

How, one might argue, is this perspective different from families' accepting that their adolescent with disabilities will be trained to work at a fast-food restaurant or choosing to place their child with disabilities in a segregated environment? Two factors intrude: the ideal of upward mobility and freedom of choice. Although we acknowledge that, in reality, many parents might indeed have few choices and that many individuals with disabilities, with other discriminated groups, may never move up a career ladder, the fact is that the milieu of individualism allows the possibility for social mobility and choice and thus for the maximization of potential.

By the same token, it might be easy to conclude that the satisficing perspective does not allow for self-determination. Indeed, it very well may not—and therein lies our argument. We must acknowledge that families' different social orientations and parental ethnotheories will have implications for their responses to the condition of disability, their perception of need for intervention, and the type of services that they might seek. An additional factor that often has an impact on families' expectations is the question of choice, which we examine next.

The Ideal of Personal Choice Western society, asserted Friedman (1996), is characterized by freedom of choice and individualism. Indeed, so entrenched in the lives of Americans is the culture of choice, from the micro level of personal choice to the macro level of political choice, by legal mandate as much as by collective social conscience (Friedman, 1996) that it has become an integral component of developmentally appropriate practice in special education instruction (Dugger-Wadsworth, 1997). For instance, Japanese and Chinese preschool teachers, viewing the instructional practices of American preschool teachers on videotape, commented on what they thought was an extraordinary emphasis on giving such young children so many choices (Tobin et al., 1989). Similarly, a major component of self-determination and other empowerment strategies is the acquisition of skills that enable people with disabilities to maximize and expand their range of life choices and to decide on, maintain, and change their life choices when necessary (Renz-Beaulaurier, 1998). Conversely, families who believe in the predominance of group identity would not endorse the need for freedom of choice for individual members ("Hmong family," 1991), much less concur with the professional emphasis placed on giving a child with disabilities choices.

The emphasis on individualism assumes that children with disabilities have rights and that they have the right to maximize their potential. These values are tied to the ideals of upward social mobility and freedom of choice. Educational programming for children with disabilities incorporates these assumptions by planning toward "a normal routine of life" including the same activities and developmental life-cycle experiences as are available to people without disabilities and by providing opportunities to children to make their own choices on these issues. Professional interactions that lack awareness of these cultural underpinnings have potential for conflict with families who may stress a satisficing perspective.

Work

In an analysis of the changing meanings and value of men's and women's work, Oughton et al. (1997) asserted that instead of defining work as an objective category, it would be more appropriate to treat work as a socially constructed category. As they stated,

> Work has an instrumental and a symbolic aspect. The instrumental aspect of work is related to the need to achieve something, whether material or nonmaterial. Work as the organisation of tasks and teams is also connected to cultural values and ideology establishing identity: gender, class, and lifestyle (Wallman, 1979). How work is codified is a cultural process, and tasks are codified according to gender relations and prestige. (Oughton et al., 1997, p. 48)

In other words, work in different cultures has different meanings and value. This section pursues this thought.

Personal Value Judged by Economic Productivity

Productivity is a crucial characteristic of capitalist economies (Cagan, 1978; Margonis, 1992). Human worth is measured in terms of economic productivity; economically "nonproductive" individuals, such as people with disabilities and older adults, are devalued. Within this social orientation, work, skills, and competence are crucial factors in the construction of individual identity. As Oughton et al. noted, "Having waged or paid work is considered in Western society as an important aspect of being an adult person because it enables the person to support him- or herself" (1997, p. 48). The association of adult identity with one's occupation is based on the ideal of social mobility (Margonis, 1992). Within this framework in which all individuals are expected to work to acquire adult status, people with disabilities must have jobs if they are to be normalized.

Definitions of Meaningful Work   Recognizing that work must be valued if it is to enhance the worker's societal worth, Brown et al. (1983) developed two criteria for meaningful work: 1) It should be essential in that if one individual did not undertake the task another person would have to, and 2) it should be paid. These precepts are underscored in the vocational option for people with disabilities—supported employment—which further emphasizes that the jobs be acquired through open competition (Shafer & Rangasamy, 1995).

As Harry and Kalyanpur pointed out, however, these criteria do not apply to all valued work even within the mainstream: work such as that of a housewife, "who performs needed work within the context of a reciprocal relationship based on a division of labor," and that of an entertainer or an artist, who "performs work which is, in fact, not necessary and would not have to be done by someone else" (1994, p. 156). These criteria also do not apply to entrepreneurs who create new kinds of businesses for which there was no previous demand (B. Furnish, personal communication, July 22, 1998). Furthermore, the issue of competitive employment for young adults with disabilities becomes moot when levels of unemployment are high among able-bodied family members, a finding corroborated in studies of Hispanic (Blue-Banning, 1997) and migrant (Leon, 1996; Pyecha & Ward, 1982; Rhodes, 1996) families and of White Mountain Apache (Shafer & Rangasamy, 1995) and Black (Skinner, 1989) youth. In addition, Shafer and Rangasamy (1995) pointed to the incongruence in targeting skills acquisition for certain jobs regardless of students' milieu, citing the case of Apache special education students who exited the school system and who were taught to work at fast-food restaurants when the restaurant nearest their reservation was 45 miles away. They asserted that the transition service planning for these students would have been more suited to their needs had it included skills and activities that were functional and valued within their tribal village or community, allowing their "partial participation in the spiritual activities of the community, traditional crafts, or engagement in chores around the family compound (wood gathering/chopping, bread making, herding, etc.)" (Shafer & Rangasamy, 1995, p. 65).

CONCLUSION

In the context of increasing professional responsibility for undertaking parenting tasks and eliciting parental involvement in the education of their child with disabilities, this chapter identified the cultural underpinnings in special education practice with specific reference to parenting styles. It analyzed the impact of the professional assumptions of universality and deficit on interactions with families whose parental ethnotheories may differ from the professional canon of appropriate practice. Probably the most egregious consequence is the labeling of parents as "abusive" without attempting to understand the meaning of their practices. This chapter also examined areas of potential conflict in the partnered process of developing education goals as a result of incongruent values and belief systems between parents and professionals.

5

The Posture of Cultural Reciprocity

Beth's Story

My daughter, Melanie, was diagnosed as having cerebral palsy soon after her birth. The most crucial problems were her inability to swallow or suck at birth, and, when she did begin to swallow, she would regurgitate most of her fluids. When she was 1 year old, she weighed only 9 pounds, and this continuing "failure to thrive" culminated in a critical state of electrolyte imbalance complicated by an aspiration pneumonia. This crisis led to a month's stay in the leading children's hospital in Toronto, Canada, where we were living at the time. After approximately 1 week in intensive care, her lungs were clear and her electrolytes were back in balance, but the doctors decided to keep her longer to find a solution to her vomiting.

For 3 weeks, the professional team tried a variety of thickened formulas, methods of feeding, and medications intended to mitigate the vomiting. Quantitative measures of how much she was fed and how much she regurgitated were kept, the latter by the use of an absorbent bib that was weighed before and after regurgitation. The medications did not work because they mostly came up as she vomited. Thicker or thinner fluids made no difference. Spoon feeding was quickly replaced by a nasogastric tube because she did seem to retain a bit more by this method. All details of her feeding were carefully documented and shared with me by a caring and meticulous professional team of doctors, nurses, and a nutritionist.

After about 3 weeks of minimal progress, the team and my family discussed but rejected a couple of more radical approaches: giving Melanie intramuscular injections of the medication and even inserting a stomach tube. We all agreed that these were too invasive. Finally, the doctors concluded that there was nothing more that they could do; they had tried all reasonable approaches, and, unfortunately, I would simply have to take Melanie home and keep trying.

The day before she was to be discharged, I sat at her bedside, talking anxiously with one of her nurses. I told her that I was puzzled about the fact that despite Melanie's continuing vomiting, she had actually gained 8 ounces in her month in the hospital. This was a much greater rate of weight gain than she had ever shown. Together the nurse and I wondered what the explanation could be. Suddenly, a thought occurred to her: "Wait a minute! You know, we give her tube feeds while she's sleeping at nights, and I don't think I've ever seen her vomit during her night feeds." She went over to the other nurse and asked whether she had noticed this, and she concurred: "No, I don't believe I've ever seen her wake during those feeds."

In amazement, I saw that the solution was before us: I exclaimed, "Well, then, that's what I'll do! I'll just feed her most of her fluids while she sleeps!" The next steps were simple: A nurse in the outpatient department taught me all I needed to know about inserting the nasal tube, the pediatrician prescribed a minimal dose of a nonnarcotic sedative, and the occupational therapist suggested that I pin a small mitten to Melanie's pajama shirt into which the feeding end of the tube could be tucked at night. We would leave her free of the tube during the days. I left the hospital armed with these materials and began a regimen of giving Melanie three "feeds" of sugared water per night. During the days, she ate semisolids and no more than a couple of teaspoons of juice or water. The nurses were right. Melanie never woke during her night feeds, and as the months went by I watched my frail little girl gain pound after pound. As she gained weight, she vomited less in the daytime, until, about 8 months later, just before the birth of her baby brother, Mark, I was able to stop tube feeding Melanie altogether. In the days, she drank juice or small amounts of water from a bottle and never again needed to have the hated tube inserted in her nose.

I have never forgotten my amazement that this professional team, in their efforts to quantify and measure the effects of their efforts, had failed to note a simple fact that had not been anticipated in their interventions. The nurses, who would have been the ones to observe the pattern directly, had been instructed to weigh and measure Melanie's vomiting but not asked whether there were differential patterns between day and night or to consider the treatment implications of such patterns.

I can interpret this only as an example of "professionalism" that had been reduced to "technicianism"—the following of instructions without making an effort to engage in individual problem solving or hypothesis testing. The rest of the professional team, who might have noted that their failure-to-thrive patient was thriving better than usual, did not think to ask whether this improvement might represent a meaningful pattern. I suspect that the emphasis on categorical recording of an intervention and on what Hall (1983) referred to as "low context" communication reduced the likelihood that these professionals would note the unanticipated event or ask the unanticipated question. I believe that truly reflective practitioners would have done so.

Finally, the story teaches a crucial lesson about parent–professional communication: The everyday knowledge of a parent can be as important as the scientific measures and theories of the professional. As a parent, I had intimate knowledge of my child's usual rate of weight gain, I had an overwhelming need to solve the problem, and I had the will to seek and implement solutions that may never have been suggested in the textbook.

This chapter presents the posture of cultural reciprocity as a method of inquiry for professionals to reflect on their practices and question the assumptions of the field. The chapter consists of four parts: the need for a posture of cultural reciprocity, the four steps of the posture, key features of the posture, and applications of the posture.

THE NEED FOR A POSTURE OF CULTURAL RECIPROCITY

Our culture is our worldview. It is what helps us to make sense of most of what we know. It is so much a part of us that, like fish in water, we are unaware of how totally it envelops us. Awareness of "cultural differences," then, is the recognition that the way we act and what we believe in can be different from the way other people act or what other people believe in. However, when we are talking about issues such as disability, which, as we have seen in previous chapters, are so open to varying interpretation, cultural awareness needs to go beyond the mere acknowledgment of what often amounts to little more than stereotypical characteristics about particular communities. As Skrtic suggested, professionals need to go through a process of introspection and inquiry that "not only questions the assumptions of the field [of special education] but also forces professionals to confront the contradictions between their values and practices" (1991, p. 42).

Using the framework that was developed by Delpit (1995) to describe levels of racial discrimination, we propose that there are three levels of cultural awareness: overt, covert, and subtle. The overt level is the awareness of obvious differences, such as language or manner of dress. These differences often are external and therefore expected; their very expectedness makes it easier to accommodate to them. When dealing with families from culturally diverse backgrounds, most mainstream professionals are aware of the more explicit aspects of cultural differences and the need for sensitivity to these differences. Indeed, the provision of an interpreter for non–English-speaking families is the most common adaptive practice. Other culturally sensitive practices include arranging for child care, arranging for transportation, and holding the meetings at a place and a time that are convenient to the participants.

Because these universalistic strategies are based on certain stereotypical assumptions about families' needs, however, they may neither respond to families' varying levels of acculturation or need nor change the power dynamics of the interaction in favor of the family. For instance, in the early 1980s, Brazilian immigrants to Boston must have been surprised when they were provided with Spanish-speaking interpreters by local social services agencies, who had quite overlooked the fact that Brazilians speak Portuguese (Guerreiro, 1987).

The covert level goes a little deeper and involves an awareness of differences that cannot be recognized by outward signs, what Philips (1983) referred to as aspects of "invisible culture," such as parameters of status or interpersonal communicative styles, that require sustained contact or observation before becoming apparent. Although covert levels of awareness can help professionals achieve greater sensitivity and acceptance of differences, the effect is still limited because professionals either may not seek an explanation for the behavior, or they may find an explanation that makes sense to them but does not make sense to the families. For instance, varying cultural concepts of time can present major barriers to effective parent–professional interaction if not understood or respected. In Kalyanpur's (1998) study of a Native American parent support group, the organizer, who was Anglo American, noticed that the meetings never started until at least 30 minutes after the members arrived. Acknowledging the need for flexibility, she adjusted her schedule accordingly and applied her concept of time and punctuality to explain that the meetings started "late." To her, this explanation made sense, but she had not really understood the Native American mothers' perception of time. They did not think that the meetings were starting late. As they saw it, the support group meetings were an occasion for them to get together, and the informal interactions among them were part of the meetings.

The limitations of both overt and covert levels of awareness are obvious. In the case of the Brazilians, prior assumptions and stereotypes on the part of the professionals brought all communication to a halt. In the case of the Native Americans, had the organizer of the support group meetings sought to understand the mothers' perspectives on the purpose of the meetings, she might have come to see the first 30 minutes not as a waste of time but as an invaluable opportunity for her to get to know the participants and learn their needs. In both cases, what was needed was another, deeper level of cultural awareness: the subtle level, examined next.

The subtle level of cultural awareness involves the recognition of embedded values and beliefs that underlie our actions and the awareness that these beliefs that we have to this point taken for granted and assumed to be universal are, in fact, beliefs and values that are specific to our culture. This effort is the most challenging because identifying these features eludes us not only in the culture of others but even more so in our own culture. For instance, for years, the Wechsler Intelligence Scale for Children (WISC; Wechsler, 1991) asked questions such as, "Who discovered America?" and, "Why is a brick house better than a wooden house?" in the belief that, as a universal truth, there was only one correct answer. In the effort to measure IQ scientifically and objectively, there was no room for those students who might think that Vespucci, not Columbus, discovered America (and even that America was never "discovered") or that in an earthquake zone, a wooden house would be safer to live in.

To reach the subtle level of cultural awareness, professionals must ask themselves, "Why?" "Why do I want 21-year-old Husain to move out on his own into a group home?" "Why do I want 4-year-old Mira to feed herself?" "Why do I want Tommy to learn to read?" By reflecting on what we do and asking why we do what we do, we come to understand what our personal and/or professional values are; that is, we are no longer blind to the fact that much of what we assumed were universal truths are in fact specific to our culture. We begin to recognize the embedded values or, in other words, the cultural underpinnings of our professional knowledge. This is what

Skrtic (1995a, 1995c) referred to as critical pragmatism and what we have been referring to throughout the book

We all are aware that potential avenues for miscommunication in parent–professional interactions are legion. The situation rarely improves when the two parties come from culturally diverse groups. It is imperative that professionals recognize that much of special education policy and practice emerges from the prevailing values and ideals of the dominant mainstream—values that may not always be held by minority cultures—so that they may decrease the potential for cross-cultural dissonance.

Awareness of cultural differences provides merely the scaffolding for building collaborative relationships. Knowledge of the underlying belief and value that brings about the difference in perspective provides the reinforcing strength to the relationship. Toward this end, we have developed an approach that we call "a posture of cultural reciprocity." We suggest that professionals adopt this approach whereby they engage in explicit discussions with families regarding differential cultural values and practices, bringing to the interactions an openness of mind, the ability to be reflective in their practice, and the ability to listen to the other perspective. Furthermore, they must respect the new body of knowledge that emerges from these discussions and make allowances for differences in perspective when responding to the family's need.

FOUR STEPS OF THE POSTURE OF CULTURAL RECIPROCITY

The posture of cultural reciprocity has four guidelines by which to work. These steps are illustrated by an example from Tharp and Gallimore's (1988) study on preschool in Hawaii:

Step 1: Identify the cultural values that are embedded in the professional interpretation of a student's difficulties or in the recommendation for service.

In other words, first ask yourself, "Why?" For instance, why does it bother you that Mekhala, your Hawaiian preschooler, always interrupts you when you are reading a story to the class and then refuses to answer when you ask questions later to assess her comprehension of the story? Or, perhaps asked another way, why do you expect that Mekhala should listen without interrupting when you are reading a story to the class and then answer your questions after you are finished reading? You might find out that you believe that interrupting people is rude, and so in your culture, people wait their turn to speak, and in school, if students know the answer, then they must raise their hands quietly and wait until the teacher calls on them.

Step 2: Find out whether the family being served recognizes and values these assumptions and, if not, how their view differs from that of the professional.

Next, find out whether the family has the same belief as you do, or find out what their belief is. Mekhala's family may tell you that they do not think that interrupting is rude, that in their culture, when somebody is telling a story, it is perfectly acceptable for listeners to participate actively with embellishments, questions, and predictions.

Step 3: Acknowledge and give explicit respect to any cultural differences identified, and fully explain the cultural basis of the professional assumptions.

Explain to the family your assumptions and beliefs and how they are different from theirs. In this case, you would explain the assumptions that you make about the rules for listeners and tellers of stories and how these assumptions are different from theirs. You believe that it is rude to interrupt; they believe that it is not. You believe that Mekhala must listen to the whole story before you can assess her understanding of it; they believe that Mekhala can show you her understanding of the story with her so-called interruptions as you narrate it.

Step 4: Through discussion and collaboration, set about determining the most effective way of adapting professional interpretations or recommendations to the value system of this family.

Together you work out an alternative solution that is acceptable to you and that does not compromise the family's beliefs. In Mekhala's case, both you and the family agree that you want two outcomes: 1) that you, as the teacher be able to assess Mekhala's comprehension of a story and 2) that Mekhala learn that in mainstream society, it is considered rude to interrupt. You have noticed that her so-called interruptions change the nature of the storytelling session from a teacher-directed approach to a more open-ended, free-flowing, student-centered format and that when students actively participate in the simultaneous construction and analysis of a story, you achieve your own goals for them: that they learn to use higher order thinking skills and that you do not have to think up questions that do that. You also notice that in other contexts—for example, when you are giving directions—Mekhala does not interrupt—or not any more than the other students, anyway—so with a little additional reinforcement, she will learn this very important rule of interpersonal communication in the mainstream culture.

KEY FEATURES OF THE
POSTURE OF CULTURAL RECIPROCITY

The posture of cultural reciprocity has five key features that make it eminently suited to the purpose of building effective parent–professional collaboration.

Goes Beyond Awareness of Differences to Self-Awareness

Developing collaborative relationships is not just a question of implementing some steps toward understanding each other when the potential for misunderstanding arises but also a constant awareness of self and others (Harry, 1992b). Furthermore, acknowledgment of a difference in perspective is insufficient without the nonjudgmental realization of the worldview behind it.

Schön (1983) wrote of the need for us to be reflective practitioners and to recognize that we are fallible and that being experts in our respective fields does not mean that we have all of the answers. He suggested that relationships between practitioners and their clients be interactive so that practitioners become aware not only of themselves and their appreciative systems (their religious, moral, political, and social ideals; social and cultural environment; and professional socialization) but also of that of others. The posture of cultural reciprocity is informed by Schön's model of the reflective practitioner.

Aims for Subtle Levels of Awareness of Differences

The posture of cultural reciprocity goes beyond recognizing overt differences to understanding cultural values that underlie professional assumptions and families' responses. As mentioned previously, culturally sensitive strategies that respond to stereotypes, although useful, are insufficient. So, too, are strategies that are based on more specific knowledge of the family's values but without an understanding of the family's point of view. Here is an example from Maya's experience: A preschool teacher scheduled a meeting with the parents of her Afghani student. She knew that many Muslims believe that women should be modest and not show their legs or arms, so she wore a long skirt and a long-sleeved blouse for the occasion. Even though her decision was based on a stereotype about Muslims, it was a courteous and thoughtful gesture; as expected, it earned her goodwill and started things off well.

The teacher told the Afghani mother that her son refused to help clean up after play and meals. The mother's response was,

"Yes, after all, he is a boy. And we don't ask boys to do that." The teacher responded politely, "Well, I understand that, but in my class everybody has to do their share and helping clean up is part of that." When the mother said nothing to this, the teacher believed that the matter was resolved. Weeks later, however, the boy still refused to clean up.

The story may have had a different ending had the teacher sought to understand the cultural values that underlay her professional assumptions and the mother's response and ask herself, "Why?" Why does she expect all of the children to do their share? Maybe it is because she shares the values of most Americans, and she believes in equality and wants to treat everybody equally. Maybe she also believes in another cherished American value, that of independence, and wants all of the children to become independent and do things for themselves, such as clean up after meals or play.

Why, then, does the mother from Afghanistan not ask her son to clean up? Maybe it is because she shares the values of *her* culture. So maybe she believes in value inequality, whereby every individual's role and status is predetermined and cleaning up traditionally has been something that women do. Perhaps she also cherishes the value of interdependence and cooperation whereby having to depend on somebody to do something for you is not devaluing. By asking why, professionals understand themselves and the families whom they serve and thus are in a better position to develop mutually acceptable interventions. Perhaps if the preschool teacher had clarified these embedded assumptions, the mother might have been persuaded to allow her son to acquire skills for success in the mainstream preschool environment while maintaining his own traditions at home.

Has Universal Applicability

We do not think that the posture of cultural reciprocity should be narrowly interpreted as a four-step strategy that is applicable only to specific contexts (i.e., parent–professional interactions in which the parties might belong to different cultural groups). Indeed, the basic construct from which the posture emerges—that communication involves listening to and respecting both perspectives—has universal applicability. By deliberately using the word *posture* to mean a stance or a position, we advocate the need for professionals to internalize the values of reciprocity, respect, and collaboration. To paraphrase Schön (1983), reflective practice should become a way of life for professionals and not be just an 8-hour syndrome.

Avoids Stereotyping

Through the internalization of the values of reciprocity, respect, and collaboration, the posture of cultural reciprocity avoids the trap of stereotypical solutions by investigating each situation as unique. Families may have differing reasons for the same behavior. For instance, parents' silence at individualized education program (IEP) meetings and similar forms of nonparticipation of minority families in the decision-making process for their child occurs for various reasons, including mistrust, discomfort with direct questioning regarding sensitive topics, fear of appearing incompetent and ignorant, deference to authority, and feelings of defiance and frustration at being silenced (Harry & Kalyanpur, 1994). The posture of cultural reciprocity enables professionals to understand each family's reasons for their silence or other specific behavior.

Ensures that Both Parents and Professionals Are Empowered

The posture of cultural reciprocity enables both parties to engage in a dialogue whereby each learns from the other. For instance, in the process of learning to manage a class of 4-year-old Haitian children, Ballenger (1994) learned about Haitian cultural ways and to query the assumptions that shaped her own experience as a North American teacher. Ballenger, a middle-income, Anglo American, noticed that her students would not respond when she told them, "If you don't clean up, you won't get a snack." She told a child whose mother had left him that she understood that he missed his mother but that he still needed to share his toys; it made not the slightest difference in his behavior.

Reflecting on her practice of asking the students to become responsible for their own behavior and to make their own moral choices, she became aware of "the powerful individualism underlying the approach [she] characterized as typical of herself and many North American teachers" (Ballenger, 1994, p. 207). Conversely, through several conversations with the parents of the children and the Haitian teachers at the school, she discovered that they would tell a child, "We don't do that," and make the child accountable to his family, even the entire community, for his behavior. She began to recognize the strong Haitian understanding that an entire extended family, as well as many people in the community, are involved in a child's upbringing and that moral choices, such as showing respect for parents and other adults and obedience to God, are predetermined.

Ballenger then presented her interpretations to the Haitian teachers and families of the children and asked them to reflect on the two cultures. Many said that although they wanted to maintain the Haitian emphasis on family unity and accountability, they thought that their children would benefit from the values of the North American culture if allowed to make their own moral choices. For example, one mother stated that although she continued to see respect as a value that she needed to impart to her children, she realized that there might be other ways to teach respect. In response, Ballenger developed what she referred to as "a mélange of styles," combining the Haitian teachers' and parents' form of verbal disciplining to emphasize communal accountability with mainstream methods that offered children opportunities to make their own choices, and she found that she was effective in managing the children's behavior. We contend that professionals in disability-related fields can be similarly effective as they not only learn more about the culture of the families whom they serve but also understand more of their own.

APPLICATIONS OF THE POSTURE OF CULTURAL RECIPROCITY

In this section, we use examples cited in previous chapters to illustrate how the posture of cultural reciprocity may be applied in interactions between parents and professionals of culturally diverse backgrounds. We have chosen examples that represent the core American values discussed in the first part of this book and examine them in the context of the posture of cultural reciprocity to see how the outcome might change when the posture is applied. However, our interpretation of which and how many values are embedded in each vignette does not preclude the possibility of alternative explanations or interpretations.

Kou: "A Sign of Grace"

In 1991, social workers in Fresno, California, wanted 7-year-old Kou, who is Hmong, to undergo corrective surgery on his two clubfeet ("Hmong family," 1991). We can easily recognize the basis for their recommendation because a clubfoot is a disabling and, therefore, stigmatizing condition in the United States. According to Kou's parents, however, his condition was "a sign of good luck" and that Kou was born with clubfeet so that "a warrior ancestor whose own feet were wounded in battle could be released from a sort of spiritual entrapment" ("Hmong family," 1991, p. 16). Therefore, they opposed the operation because they feared that it would bring disaster on the entire Hmong community. The case went to court, and the judge ruled in favor of the parents.

Had the social workers adopted the posture of cultural reciprocity, perhaps the court need not have intervened. At the first step, the social workers would have identified to Kou's parents their reasons for recommending surgery and recognized that in the mainstream culture, a clubfoot is a physical condition that is perceived to be disabling and stigmatizing. Informed by core American values, they believed that Kou had rights as an individual to seek treatment.

Moving to the second step, through conversations with the Hmong family, the social workers would have learned that the same condition is a sign of grace in the Hmong culture and that surgery could bring disaster to the entire community. They would have recognized two opposing values embedded within this perspective: 1) the belief among many Hmong families that spirit, mind, and body are interconnected and that "spiritual unwellness" can result from physical illness (Conquergood, 1988; Fadiman, 1997; Meyers, 1992) and 2) group status and coherence. Asian family structures are close-knit, extensive, and interdependent: Although communities are responsible for the social and mental well-being of each individual, by the same token, every member has social obligations and duties to his or her community that supersede the rights of the individual (Lee, 1996). Within this framework, given that the well-being of the entire Hmong community might be jeopardized by the individualistic act of a single member, Kou's family did not believe that he had either individual rights or personal choice in the matter.

At the third step, the social workers would have acknowledged to the family these differences in perspectives as they learned more about Hmong traditions. Perhaps they might have asked whether Kou's family wished to acculturate and adopt mainstream values and beliefs. The social workers may have recalled some traditions within their own families that were carried over by the first generation and maintained by succeeding generations, and they might have talked about the decisions that they made about letting go or keeping those values that conflicted with mainstream values.

At the fourth step, the dialogue might have concluded with the social workers' telling the family that if they wished to maintain their traditions, then Kou would continue to be perceived as special within their family and community but that the family must understand the long-term consequences for becoming acculturated if they decided against the surgery. The family thus would have been empowered to make an informed decision for themselves. Perhaps because Kou's family decided that they wanted to maintain their traditions and did not opt for the surgery, the social workers not only would have agreed to honor their choice and tradition but also would have come to realize that although Kou's condition is a disability that makes him different, it need not necessarily be a stigmatizing difference.

Rani: "She's Becoming Rebellious"

In Kalyanpur's (1998) study, Rani was a 22-year-old Native American woman with moderate developmental delay who lived with her parents on the reservation. Since Rani graduated from school the previous year, having received special education services all through, her parents had been trying to find something for Rani to do. They did not want Rani to leave the reservation to find work, but jobs were hard to find on the reservation. Then a university professor told them of a new series of courses that were being offered at the local community college and that focused on developing independent living skills for people with disabilities. Because Rani's sister attended this community college and would be both companion and escort for Rani, her parents enrolled her in the program. During the first semester, on the professor's advice, Rani took a course on money management and one on self-advocacy, called "The New You," designed to help Rani become assertive and aware of her rights. The professor hoped that the latter would encourage Rani to get away from her overprotective parents and seek supported employment and living arrangements that were available outside the reservation, so he was disappointed when, at the end of the semester, Rani's parents decided to pull her out of the program because "she had learnt to talk back to them and her father did not like that" (Kalyanpur, 1998, p. 321). They believed that "The New You" course was making Rani "rebellious."

In applying the first step of the posture of cultural reciprocity, the professor would have identified that the reason for his recommending the "The New You" course to Rani lay in the high value placed on a person's becoming financially and physically/geographically independent as a transition to adulthood within the mainstream culture (Repetto & Correa, 1996; Shafer & Rangasamy, 1995). As per his training, in his perspective, Rani, at 22, needed to move out of her parents' home just as any typical adult would. Group homes were developed on the principle of normalization, which recognized that moving out of the parental home is a milestone of adulthood for people without disabilities and should be a life goal for people with disabilities as well (Racino & Taylor, 1993).

Had the professor engaged in a dialogue with Rani's parents, he might have discovered that although moving out may be an option as Native American children become adults (Clay, 1992), it does not always entail leaving the reservation—indeed, Rani's six older sisters live within proximity of their parents on the same reservation—and that the family places an emphasis on interdependence and on "looking after one's own" (Kalyanpur, 1998, p. 320). Furthermore, Rani's disability gives her special status, and there is no stigma to her not moving out. On the contrary, her family assumes that she will continue to remain with her parents for as long as they can look after her, after which she would move into the care of one of her sisters.

At the third step, the professor and Rani's parents would have described their seemingly separate visions for Rani's future and begun to identify some commonalities in them: They all want Rani to become as financially independent as possible, and they agree that supported employment on the reservation would be a comfortable solution.

For the fourth step, they might have put their heads together and come up with the idea that her parents build an extension to their home and set up Rani in her own store where she could sell sundry items to the commuters who drive through the reservation on their way to and from work and to the children at the reservation school. For the professor, this notion would be based on his belief in self-determination and the need to provide opportunities for individuals with disabilities to become independent. For the parents, this notion would be based on their belief in "looking after one's own," an integral aspect of the caring and cooperative nature of their culture.

Annie: "The Good Mother"

In Kalyanpur and Rao's (1991) study, Annie, an African American mother of two toddlers, was reported to child protection services by a social worker, Caroline, for spanking her children. The single act, performed with the best intentions, had several unfortunate consequences. Annie became bitter not only because she was accused of being an abusive parent but also because of what she saw as a betrayal of trust by Caroline, and, as a result, the relationship between the two women deteriorated. She decided that she could not trust any professionals, no matter how friendly they might be. On her part, Caroline remained convinced of Annie's self-admitted "crime" and saw no need to change her mind about Annie's parenting skills.

If, instead, Caroline had applied the posture of cultural reciprocity, then she first would have asked herself why it bothers her that Annie spanks her children or, perhaps, why she expects Annie to bring up her children without spanking them. She would have realized that in her professional training, she was taught that child maltreatment is any parental behavior that places a child in imminent danger of serious harm and that she is required to issue a report when circumstances lead her to have reasonable cause to suspect that a child has been maltreated (Mahoney, 1995). She would have realized that, as Hong and Hong (1991) pointed out, social standards for the treatment of children are biased in favor of selected segments of society, specifically the Caucasian middle income and those in positions of social and professional power: A middle-income Anglo American herself, she would have realized that she, too, prefers verbal forms of disciplining over physical disciplinary practices and sees spanking, a type of corporal punishment, as physical abuse (Janek, 1992). Furthermore, under the assumption that "good" parenting is culture-free, she has been trained to recognize certain child-rearing practices such as verbal disciplining as "good" and physical disciplinary practices such as spanking a child as "wrong" rather than as different. Thus, she concluded that Annie is an inadequate, even bad, parent.

Next, investigating whether Annie recognizes and values these assumptions and, if not, how her view differs, Caroline would have questioned her and learned that although Annie believes that spanking is a permissible disciplinary technique and practices it, she makes a distinction between "beating" and "spanking." Annie is fully aware that beating is an abusive form of punishment. Furthermore, Caroline would have discovered that according to Annie, spanking is a sign of good parenting and that a spanking when the occasion demands will help her children to grow up responsibly. Annie would have clarified that she uses spanking only on occasion and then, too, as a last resort. Caroline would have acknowledged that the reasonable use of corporal punishment is not illegal (Howing & Wodarski, 1992) and that Annie is familiar with nonphysical and verbal forms of discipline as well.

In the third step, Caroline would have explained her beliefs to Annie and how they are different from hers. She would have told Annie that she has been trained to believe that spanking is "wrong" and that spanking is not an appropriate parenting practice. She would have acknowledged Annie's perspective that spanking is a nonabusive way to discipline her children and respected Annie's desire to be a good mother to her children. They would have exchanged stories: Caroline would talk about her training, how she was taught to ask questions when she saw a bruise on a child, even perhaps how she was disciplined as a child herself. Annie would talk about her hopes for her children and describe what it is like to be living on the brink as a low-income single parent with no guarantees of a less precarious life for her children.

In the final step, Caroline and Annie would have pondered the two points of view expressed. Were they so completely incompatible that it would be impossible to find a middle ground and work out a solution that is acceptable to Caroline and does not compromise Annie's beliefs? Surely not. By the time Annie and Caroline exchanged stories, they would have as likely as not built a deeper understanding of each other, each recognizing why the other believes what she does. Caroline would have recognized that parenting styles differ and that these differences do not constitute deficits: They certainly do not mean that a person is a good or a bad parent. She would have recognized that Annie, in fact, is a good parent and that her values and expectations for her children are similar to those of any parent. This new knowledge would have empowered Caroline. In turn, Caroline's acknowledgment of Annie's competence as a parent and her increased trust in Annie's judgment would have allowed Caroline to introduce ideas that Annie could *add* to her repertoire of skills, thus empowering Annie.

Nancy: "Their Culture Isn't Helping Them"

Like the other professionals in Kalyanpur's (1998) study, Nancy, a child psychologist, was trained in the dominant tradition of technical rationalism, which expects the professional to define both the problem and the solution (Schön, 1983). When she was hired to provide developmental screening and diagnostic evaluation services to Native American preschool children, she applied her expertise and prior knowledge about the community to identify what she termed a "language delay" in the children, even though they spoke their native language and some were even bilingual. Her diagnosis of the problem was

> If they want to compete in the mainstream, then they must learn to be more verbal. My emphasis would be on language development. Getting the mothers to see the importance of talking to their child from an early age [and] getting the child interested in reading. (Kalyanpur, 1998, p. 322)

According to her, the "language delay" was a "cultural deficit" that justified the need for a preschool program:

> It's because of the culture. The children aren't encouraged to talk very much. So their receptive language is very good, but not their expressive. But it's difficult to tell the parents. I mean, how do you tell them that their culture isn't helping their children? (Kalyanpur, 1998, p. 322)

In applying the posture of cultural reciprocity, Nancy would come to understand that her thinking was informed by the framework of the "cultural deficit" model (Wright, Saleeby, Watts, & Lecca, 1983). First, she had measured the language development of the children by a yardstick of the mainstream culture: emphasis on verbal skills (Lipka, 1991; McCarty, Lynch, Wallace, & Benally, 1991). Then, finding the children's proficiency in English somewhat wanting, she had assumed that the minority culture deprived children of the opportunity to learn language skills. Furthermore, implicit in her argument was the cultural assumption that becoming "mainstreamed" was a desired, even a necessary, outcome—an assumption commonly held among many professionals (Henze & Vanett, 1993).

Moving to the second step to discover whether the Native Americans recognized and valued these assumptions, Nancy would learn of alternative culture-specific language development practices. The mothers would tell her that in their culture, learning occurs by observing (Gray & Cosgrove, 1985); one mother would describe how she "learned as she watched" her child receive physical therapy. Nancy might observe that parent–child interactions were physical, warm, and frequent but nonverbal. At the parent support group meetings, the children would run to their mothers, who would hold them silently, almost absent-mindedly, while continuing to speak to the adult, before letting them go. At the end of the meetings, the children would not regale their mothers with stories of what they did or the toys with which they played. Instead, they would allow themselves to be bundled into their coats without protest while the mothers spoke over their heads to each other.

Nancy might apply her professional knowledge about research in the field to recall documented differences in sociolinguistic styles in Native American cultures (Lipka, 1991; McCarty et al., 1991; Philips, 1983). For instance, unlike in the mainstream, interpersonal communication modes among the Yup'ik include silences, modeled behavior, a parsimonious use of words, and intentional ignoring (Lipka, 1991). And when an inquiry-based curriculum that

imitated patterns of learning for Navajo students outside the classroom was implemented within the school, the students responded
actively in their second language (McCarty et al., 1991).

Next, Nancy would acknowledge that just because the Native
American mothers did not talk directly to their children does not
mean that the children do not acquire language and that the notion
that a "difference" was a "deficit" was wrong. Perhaps she might recall that, until the 1940s, the Protestant ethic that "children should
be seen and not heard" prevailed in many mainstream families
(Butchart, 1998). She would ask the mothers whether they intended
to send their children to the mainstream school outside the reservation; if so, then she would let them know what the mainstream expectations for academic achievement would be.

The final step might lead Nancy into a discussion with the
mothers about the possibility of using the preschool program or creating other group opportunities in which both she and the children
(with the mothers on hand) could learn the other's sociolinguistic
style. In her study of African American students, Delpit (1995)
noted that when students received both direct instruction on Standard English and other sociolinguistic aspects of the mainstream
culture and opportunities to use African American Vernacular English during concept acquisition, they were more successful acade-
mically. Applying this knowledge, Nancy and the mothers could
decide to give the children opportunities to develop 1) socialization
and cognitive skills considered important within the Native American culture, 2) reading and other academic readiness skills using
the Native American style of interaction with which they would be
familiar, and 3) socialization skills considered important within the
mainstream culture.

CONCLUSION

Implementing the posture of cultural reciprocity is not easy. Probably the biggest barrier to implementation is time. As professionals
battle to find time to send just a quick note home to parents every
day or call on a regular basis to touch base with clients, it may seem
unrealistic to expect anybody to make the time to get to know each
other, let alone engage in dialogue. To counter this argument, we refer to a point made previously: The posture of cultural reciprocity
cannot be seen as a bag of tricks to be pulled out during situations
of conflict or in emergencies but almost as a value that is internalized and applied in all contexts. If we seek to understand ourselves
and the families whom we serve at every interaction, however

small, then the task will seem less onerous. If when we send that quick note or make that telephone call we reflect on our action and ask ourselves why we are saying what we are saying, then we will be more likely to understand when the families do not say what we want them to say and more likely to make the effort to learn why.

Another barrier is the mistaken belief that only professionals from minority cultures can work with families from minority cultures. There is no evidence that professionals who do belong to the same culture as their clients are any more successful at accomplishing collaborative relationships than those who do not; on the contrary, as studies (Harry, 1992b; Ladson-Billings, 1994) indicated, the best examples of collaborative relationships can occur with professionals who have little or no affiliation with the culture of the families. The issue is not that we must have had the same experiences in terms of culture, ethnic background, race, socioeconomic status, or gender as the families we serve—because we cannot—but that we have the willingness to learn about and understand their experiences, that we are willing to understand how our own experiences have shaped us, and that we respect and accept these differences in our various experiences.

References

Adam, B. (1995). *Timewatch: The social analysis of time.* Cambridge, England: Polity Press.

Algozzine, B. (1977). The emotionally disturbed child: Disturbed or disturbing? *American Journal of Abnormal Child Psychology, 5,* 205–211.

Apple, M.W., & Beane, J.A. (Eds.). (1995). *Democratic schools.* Alexandria, VA: Association for Supervision and Curriculum Development.

Arden, S. (1987). Onondaga six nation territory. *National Geographic, 172,* 370–403.

Artiles, A.J. (1998). The dilemma of difference: Enriching the disproportionality discourse with theory and context. *Journal of Special Education, 32,* 32–36.

Artiles, A.J., & Trent, S.C. (1994). Overrepresentation of minority students in special education: A continuing debate. *Journal of Special Education, 27*(4), 410–437.

Athans, M. (1998, January 20). Illiteracy among girls comes to light. *Lawrence Journal-World,* 5A.

Attneave, C. (1982). American Indians and Alaska Native families: Emigrants in their own homeland. In M. McGoldrick, J.K. Pearce, & J. Giordano (Eds.), *Ethnicity and family therapy* (pp. 55–83). New York: Guilford Press.

Ballenger, C. (1994). Because you like us: The language of control. *Harvard Educational Review, 62,* 199–208.

Banks, J.A. (1997a). Multicultural education: Characteristics and goals. In J.A. Banks & C.A. McGee Banks (Eds.), *Multicultural education: Issues and perspectives* (3rd ed., pp. 3–31). Needham Heights, MA: Allyn & Bacon.

Banks, J.A. (1997b). *Teaching strategies for ethnic studies* (6th ed.). Needham Heights, MA: Allyn & Bacon.

Barton, L., & Tomlinson, S. (Eds.). (1984). *Special education and social interests.* New York: Nichols.

Bean, G., & Thorburn, M. (1995). Mobilising parents of children with disabilities in Jamaica and the English speaking Caribbean. In B. O'Toole & R. McConkey (Eds.), *Innovations in developing countries for people with disabilities* (pp. 105–120). Chorley, England: Lisieux Hall, in association with Associazione Italiana Amici di Raoul Follereau.

Behr, S.K., & Murphy, D.L. (1993). Research progress and promise: The role of perceptions in cognitive adaptation to disability. In A.P. Turnbull, J.M.

Patterson, S.K. Behr, D.L. Murphy, J.G. Marquis, & M.J. Blue-Banning (Eds.), *Cognitive coping, families, and disability* (pp. 151–163). Baltimore: Paul H. Brookes Publishing Co.

Bennett, A.T. (1988). Gateways to powerlessness: Incorporating Hispanic deaf children and families into formal schooling. *Disability, Handicap, and Society, 3,* 119–151.

Bernheimer, L.P., & Keogh, B.K. (1995). Weaving interventions into the fabric of everyday life: An approach of family assessment. *Topics in Early Childhood Special Education, 15,* 415–433.

Bérubé, M. (1996). *Life as we know it: A father, a family, and an exceptional child.* New York: Pantheon.

Beyer, L.E. (1998). "Uncontrollable students eventually become unmanageable": The politics of classroom discipline. In R.E. Butchart & B. McEwan (Eds.), *Classroom discipline in American schools: Problems and possibilities for democratic education* (pp. 51–84). Albany: State University of New York Press.

Bibb, A., & Casimir, G.J. (1996). Haitian families. In M. McGoldrick, J. Giordano, & J.K. Pearce (Eds.), *Ethnicity and family therapy* (2nd ed., pp. 97–111). New York: Guilford Press.

Biklen, D. (1974). *Let our children go: An organizing manual for advocates and parents.* Syracuse, NY: Human Policy Press.

Blue-Banning, M.J. (1997). *The transition of Hispanic adolescents with disabilities to adulthood: Parent and professional perspectives.* Unpublished doctoral dissertation, University of Kansas, Lawrence.

Bogdan, R., & Knoll, J. (1995). The sociology of disability. In E.L. Meyen & T.M. Skrtic (Eds.), *Special education and student disability: An introduction. Traditional, emerging, and alternative perspectives* (4th ed., pp. 609–674). Denver: Love Publishing.

Borthwick-Duffy, S.A., Eyman, R.K., & White, J.F. (1987). Client characteristics and residential placement patterns. *American Journal of Mental Deficiency, 92*(1), 24–30.

Bowers, C.A. (1984). *The promise of theory: Education and the politics of cultural change.* New York: Longman.

Bowers, C.A. (1995). *Educating for an ecologically sustainable culture: Rethinking moral education, creativity, intelligence, and other modern orthodoxies.* Albany: State University of New York Press.

Bowles, S., & Gintis, H. (1976). *Schooling in capitalist America: Educational reform and contradictions of economic life.* New York: Basic Books.

Brady, M.P., & Anderson, D.D. (1983). Some issues in the implementation of P.L. 94-142 in the Pacific Basin Territories. *Education, 103*(3), 259–269.

Bredekamp, S. (1997). Foreword. In C.H. Hart, D.C. Burts, & R. Charlesworth (Eds.), *Integrated curriculum and developmentally appropriate practice: Birth to age eight* (pp. xv–xvii). Albany: State University of New York Press.

Bromwich, R. (1997). *Working with families and their infants at risk: A perspective after twenty years of experience.* Austin, TX: PRO-ED.

Brown, L., Shiraga, B., Ford, A., Nisbet, J., Van Deventer, P., Sweet, M., York, J., & Loomis, R. (1983). Teaching severely handicapped students to perform meaningful work in nonsheltered vocational environments. In R.

Morris & B. Blatt (Eds.), *Perspectives in special education: State of the art.* Glenview, IL: Scott, Foresman.

Bruininks, R.H., & Lakin, K.C. (Eds.). (1985). *Living and learning in the least restrictive environment.* Baltimore: Paul H. Brookes Publishing Co.

Bullivant, B.M. (1993). Culture: Its nature and meaning for educators. In J. Banks & C. McGee-Banks (Eds.), *Multicultural education: Issues and perspectives* (2nd ed., pp. 29–47). Needham Heights, MA: Allyn & Bacon.

Burger, A.L. (1977). Chinese-Americans: Another minority. In J. Wortis (Ed.), *Mental retardation and developmental disabilities: An annual review* (pp. 274–287). New York: Brunner/Mazel.

Burian, B.K., & Slimp, P.A.O. (1994). Multiple role relationships during internship: Consequences and recommendations. *Professional Psychology, Research and Practice, 25,* 39–46.

Buriel, R., Mercado, R., Rodriguez, J., & Chavez, J.M. (1991). Mexican-American disciplinary practices and attitudes towards child maltreatment: A comparison of foreign- and native-born mothers. *Hispanic Journal of Behavioral Sciences, 13*(1), 78–94.

Butchart, R.E. (1998). Punishments, penalties, prizes, and procedures: A history of discipline in U.S. schools. In R.E. Butchart & B. McEwan (Eds.), *Classroom discipline in American schools: Problems and possibilities for democratic action* (pp. 19–50). Albany: State University of New York Press.

Cagan, E. (1978). Individualism, collectivism, and radical educational reform. *Harvard Educational Review, 48,* 227–266.

Cameron, G., & Vanderwoerd, J. (with Peirson, L.). (1997). Parent training programs in child welfare. In *Protecting children and supporting families: Promising programs and organizational realities* (pp. 151–170). New York: Aldine de Gruyter.

Carpenter, B. (1997). Empowering parents: The use of the parent as researcher paradigm in early intervention. *Journal of Child and Family Studies, 6,* 391–398.

Chan, S. (1986). Parents of exceptional Asian children. In M.K. Kitano & P.C. Chinn (Eds.), *Exceptional Asian children and youth* (pp. 36–53). Reston, VA: Council for Exceptional Children.

Chung, D.K. (1992a). Asian cultural commonalities: A comparison with mainstream American culture. In S.M. Furuto, R. Biswas, D.K. Chung, K. Murase, & F. Ross-Sheriff (Eds.), *Social work practice with Asian Americans* (pp. 27–44). Thousand Oaks, CA: Sage Publications.

Chung, D.K. (1992b). The Confucian model of social transformation. In S.M. Furuto, R. Biswas, D.K. Chung, K. Murase, & F. Ross-Sheriff (Eds.), *Social work practice with Asian Americans* (pp. 125–142). Thousand Oaks, CA: Sage Publications.

Clay, J.A. (1992). Native American independent living. *Rural Special Education Quarterly, 11*(1), 41–50.

Cloud, N. (1993). Language, culture, and disability: Implications for instruction and teacher preparation. *Teacher Education and Special Education, 16,* 60–72.

Collins, R., & Camblin, L.D. (1983). The politics and science of learning disability classification: Implications for Black children. *Contemporary Education, 54*(2), 113–118.

Connery, A.R. (1987). *A description and comparison of Native American and Anglo parents' knowledge of their handicapped children's rights.*

Unpublished doctoral dissertation, Northern Arizona University, Flagstaff.

Conquergood, D. (1988). Health theatre in a Hmong refugee camp: Performance, communication, and culture. *The Drama Review, 32*(3), 174–208.

Conrad, P. (1976). *Identifying hyperactive children.* Lexington, MA: Lexington/D.C. Health.

Cooney, M.H. (1995, Spring). Readiness for school or for school culture? *Childhood Education,* 164–166.

Coots, J.J. (1998). Family resources and parent participation in schooling activities for their children with developmental delays. *Journal of Special Education, 31,* 498–520.

Correa, V.I. (1989). Involving culturally diverse families in the educational process. In S.H. Fradd & M.J. Weismantel (Eds.), *Meeting the needs of culturally and linguistically different students: A handbook for educators* (pp. 130–144). Boston: College-Hill Press.

Correa, V.I. (1992). Cultural accessibility of services for culturally diverse clients with disabilities and their families. *Rural Special Education Quarterly, 11*(2), 6–12.

Cross, T. (1995). Developing a knowledge base to support cultural competence. *Family Resource Coalition Report, 14*(3 & 4), 17–18.

Cunningham, K., Cunningham, K., & O'Connell, J.C. (1986). Impact of differing cultural perceptions on special education service delivery. *Rural Special Education Quarterly, 8,* 2–8.

Cutler, B.C. (1993). *You, your child, and "special education": A guide to making the system work.* Baltimore: Paul H. Brookes Publishing Co.

Danseco, E.R. (1997a). *Building bridges: African-American mothers' and teachers' ethnotheories on child development, child problems, and home–school relations for children with and without disabilities.* Unpublished doctoral dissertation, University of Maryland, College Park.

Danseco, E.R. (1997b). Parental beliefs on childhood disability: Insights on culture, child development, and intervention. *International Journal of Disability, Development, and Education, 44*(1), 41–52.

Das, M. (1995). Tough decisions: One family's experiences crosses cultures and continents. *Volta Voices, 2*(3), 5–7.

DeGangi, G., Wietlisbach, S., & Royeen, C. (1994). The impact of culture and socioeconomic status on family–professional collaboration: Challenges and solutions. *Topics in Early Childhood Special Education, 14,* 503–521.

Delpit, L.D. (1995). *Other people's children: Cultural conflicts in the classroom.* New York: New Press.

Dentler, R.A., & Hafner, A.L. (1997). *Hosting newcomers: Structuring educational opportunities for immigrant children.* New York: Teachers College Press.

Devlieger, P. (1995). Why disabled? The cultural understanding of physical disability in an African society. In B. Ingstad & S.R. Whyte (Eds.), *Disability and culture* (pp. 94–106). Berkeley: University of California Press.

deVries, M.W., & deVries, M.R. (1977). Cultural relativity of toilet training readiness: A perspective from East Africa. *Pediatrics, 60,* 170–177.

Dinnebeil, L.A., & Rule, S. (1994). Variables that influence collaboration between parents and service coordinators. *Journal of Early Intervention, 18,* 349–361.

Dorris, M. (1989). *The broken cord.* New York: HarperCollins.

Drake, S. (1997). Confronting the ultimate learning outcome: We teach who we are. In T.E. Jennings (Ed.), *Restructuring for integrative education: Multiple perspectives, multiple contexts* (pp. 39–52). Westport, CT: Bergin & Garvey.

Dugger-Wadsworth, D.E. (1997). The integrated curriculum and students with disabilities. In C.H. Hart, D.C. Burts, & R. Charlesworth (Eds.), *Integrated curriculum and developmentally appropriate practice: Birth to age eight* (pp. 335–362). Albany: State University of New York Press.

Dukerich, J.M., Dutton, J.E., & McCabe, D.L. (1994). The effects of professional education on values and the resolution of ethical dilemmas: Business school vs. law school students. *Journal of Business Ethics, 13,* 693–701.

Edgerton, R.B. (1970). Mental retardation in non-Western societies: Toward a cross-cultural perspective on incompetence. In H.C. Haywood (Ed.), *Sociocultural aspects of mental retardation* (pp. 523–559). New York: Appleton-Century-Crofts.

Edwards, C.P., Gandini, L., & Giovaninni, D. (1996). The contrasting developmental timetables of parents and preschool teachers in two cultural communities. In S. Harkness & C.M. Super (Eds.), *Parents' cultural belief systems: Their origins, expressions, and consequences* (pp. 270–288). New York: Guilford Press.

Edwards, M.L. (1997). Constructions of physical disability in the ancient Greek world: The community concept. In D.T. Mitchell & S.L. Snyder (Eds.), *The body and physical difference: Discourses of disability* (pp. 35–50). Ann Arbor: University of Michigan Press.

Fadiman, A. (1997). *The spirit catches you and you fall down: A Hmong child, her American doctors, and the collision of two cultures.* New York: Farrar, Straus, & Giroux.

Falicov, C.J. (1996). Mexican families. In M. McGoldrick, J. Giordano, & J.K. Pearce (Eds.), *Ethnicity and family therapy* (2nd ed., pp. 169–182). New York: Guilford Press.

Fass, P.S. (1989). *Minorities and the transformation of American education.* New York: Oxford University Press.

Ferguson, P.M. (1994). *Abandoned to their fate: Social policy and practice toward severely retarded people in America, 1820–1920.* Philadelphia: Temple University Press.

Ferguson, P.M., Ferguson, D.L., & Jones, D. (1988). Generations of hope: Parental perspectives on the transitions of their children with severe retardation from school to adult life. *Journal of The Association for Persons with Severe Handicaps, 13,* 177–187.

Figler, C.S. (1981, February). *Puerto Rican families with and without handicapped children.* Paper presented at the Council for Exceptional Children Conference on the Exceptional Bilingual Child, New Orleans, LA.

Fine, M. (1993). [Ap]parent involvement: reflections on parents, power, and urban public schools. *Teachers College Record, 94,* 682–711.

Fishlock, T. (1983). *Gandhi's children.* New York: Universe.

Forjuoh, S.N. (1995). Pattern of intentional burns to children in Ghana. *Child Abuse and Neglect, 19*(7), 837–841.

Friedman, L.M. (1990). *The republic of choice: Law, authority, and culture.* Cambridge, MA: Harvard University Press.

Friedman, L.M. (1996). Are we a litigious people? In L.M. Friedman & H.N. Scheiber (Eds.), *Legal culture and the legal profession* (pp. 53–78). Boulder, CO: Westview Press.

Friedsam, H.J. (1995, Summer). Professional education and the invention of social gerontology. *Generations: What It Means to Be a Professional in the Field of Aging*, 46–50.

Fulcher, G. (1989). *Disabling policies? A comparative approach to education policy and disability*. Philadelphia: Falmer Press.

Fulcher, G. (1996). Beyond normalisation but not Utopia. In L. Barton (Ed.), *Disability and society: Emerging issues and insights* (pp. 167–190). London: Longman.

Garcia-Preto, N. (1996). Puerto Rican families. In M. McGoldrick, J. Giordano, & J.K. Pearce (Eds.), *Ethnicity and family therapy* (2nd ed., pp. 183–199). New York: Guilford Press.

Gardner, H. (1993). *Frames of mind: The theory of multiple intelligences*. New York: Basic Books.

Garlington, J.A. (1991). *Helping dreams survive: The story of a project involving African-American families in the education of their children*. Washington, DC: National Committee for Citizens in Education.

Gibbs, B. (1993). Providing support to sisters and brothers of children with disabilities. In G.H.S. Singer & L.E. Powers (Eds.), *Families, disability, and empowerment: Active coping skills and strategies for family interventions* (pp. 343–363). Baltimore: Paul H. Brookes Publishing Co.

Gibson, M.A. (1987). Punjabi immigrants in an American high school. In G. Spindler & L. Spindler (Eds.), *Interpretive ethnography of education: At home and abroad* (pp. 281–310). Mahwah, NJ: Lawrence Erlbaum & Associates.

Giroux, H.A. (1993). *Living dangerously: Multiculturalism and the politics of difference*. New York: Lang.

Glasser, T.L. (1992). Professionalism and the derision of diversity: The case of the education of journalists. *Journal of Communication, 42*, 131–141.

Goode, D.A. (1992). Who is Bobby? Ideology and method in the discovery of a Down syndrome person's competence. In P.M. Ferguson, D.L. Ferguson, & S.J. Taylor (Eds.), *Interpreting disability: A qualitative reader* (pp. 197–212). New York: Teachers College Press.

Gould, S.J. (1981). *The mismeasure of man*. New York: Norton.

Gray, E., & Cosgrove, J. (1985). Ethnocentric perception of childrearing practices in protective services. *Child Abuse and Neglect, 9*, 389–396.

Greene, M. (1988). *The dialectic of freedom*. New York: Teachers College Press.

Groce, N.E., & Zola, I.K. (1993). Multiculturalism, chronic illness, and disability. *Pediatrics, 91*, 1048–1055.

Guerreiro, L.A. (1987). An exploratory study of home–school relations among Portuguese immigrants having handicapped children. *Contemporary Education, 58*(3), 150–154.

Gwaltney, J. (1970). *The thrice shy: Cultural accommodation to blindness*. New York: Columbia University Press.

Hadaway, N., & Marek-Schroer, M.F. (1992). Multidimensional assessment of the gifted minority student. *Roeper Review, 15*(2), 73–77.

Hahn, H. (1986). Public support for rehabilitation programs: The analysis of U.S. disability policy. *Disability, Handicap, and Society, 1*(2), 121–137.

Hall, E.T. (1981). *Beyond culture.* Garden City, NY: Anchor Press/Doubleday.

Hall, E.T. (1983). *The dance of life: The other dimension of time.* Garden City, NY: Anchor Press/Doubleday.

Haq, H. (1970). *Disability in antiquity.* New York: Philosophical Library.

Hardman, M.L., Drew, C.J., & Egan, M.W. (1999). *Human exceptionality: Society, school, and family* (6th ed.). Needham Heights, MA: Allyn & Bacon.

Hareven, T.K. (1982). American families in transition: Historical perspectives on change. In F. Walsh (Ed.), *Normal family process* (pp. 447–465). New York: Guilford Press.

Harkness, S., & Super, C.M. (1996). Introduction. In S. Harkness & C.M. Super (Eds.), *Parents' cultural belief systems: Their origins, expressions, and consequences* (pp. 1–26). New York: Guilford Press.

Harris, M. (1974). *Cows, pigs, wars, and witches: The riddles of culture.* New York: Random House.

Harry, B. (1992a). *Cultural diversity, families, and the special education system: Communication and empowerment.* New York: Teachers College Press.

Harry, B. (1992b). Developing cultural self-awareness: The first step in values clarification for early interventionists. *Topics in Early Childhood Special Education, 12,* 333–350.

Harry, B. (1992c). An ethnographic study of cross-cultural communication with Puerto Rican-American families in the special education system. *American Educational Research Journal, 29,* 471–494.

Harry, B. (1992d). Making sense of disability: Low-income, Puerto Rican parents' theories of the problem. *Exceptional Children, 59,* 27–40.

Harry, B. (1992e). Restructuring the participation of African-American parents in special education. *Exceptional Children, 59,* 123–131.

Harry, B. (1994). *The disproportionate representation of minority students in special education: Theories and recommendations.* Alexandria, VA: National Association of State Directors of Special Education.

Harry, B. (1997). Applications and misapplications of ecological principles in working with families from diverse cultural backgrounds. In J.L. Paul, M. Churton, W.C. Morse, A.J. Duchnowski, B. Epanchin, P.G. Osnes, & R.L. Smith (Eds.), *Special education practice: Applying the knowledge, affirming the values, creating the future* (pp. 156–170). Pacific Grove, CA: Brooks/Cole.

Harry, B. (1998). Parental visions of "una vida normal/a normal life": Cultural variations on a theme. In L.H. Meyer, H.-S. Park, M. Grenot-Scheyer, I.S. Schwartz, & B. Harry (Eds.), *Making friends: The influences of culture and development* (pp. 47–62). Baltimore: Paul H. Brookes Publishing Co.

Harry, B., Allen, N., & McLaughlin, M. (1995). Communication versus compliance: African-American parents' involvement in special education. *Exceptional Children, 61,* 364–377.

Harry, B., Allen, N., & McLaughlin, M. (1996). "Old-fashioned, good teachers": African American parents' views of effective early instruction. *Learning Disabilities Research and Practice, 11,* 193–201.

Harry, B., & Anderson, M.G. (1994). The disproportionate placement of African American males in special education programs: A critique of the process. *Journal of Negro Education, 63*(4), 602–620.

Harry, B., & Kalyanpur, M. (1994). Cultural underpinnings of special education: Implications for professional interactions with culturally diverse families. *Disability and Society, 9*(2), 145–165.

Harry, B., Rueda, R., & Kalyanpur, M. (1998). *From normalization to ecocultural analysis: A sociocultural approach to responsive intervention with culturally diverse families of children with disabilities.* Manuscript submitted for publication.

Heath, S.B. (1983). *Ways with words: Language, life, and work in communities and classrooms.* New York: Cambridge University Press.

Helander, B. (1995). Disability as incurable illness: Health, process, and personhood in southern Somalia. In B. Ingstad & S.R. Whyte (Eds.), *Disability and culture* (pp. 73–93). Berkeley: University of California Press.

Heller, K.A., Holtzman, W.H., & Messick, S. (1982). *Placing children in special education: A strategy for equity.* Washington, DC: National Academy Press.

Heller, T., & Factor, A. (1991). Permanency planning for adults with mental retardation living with family caregivers. *American Journal of Mental Retardation, 96*(2), 163–176.

Helms, J.E. (1992). Why is there no study of cultural equivalence in standardized cognitive ability testing? *American Psychologist, 47,* 1083–1100.

Henze, R.C., & Vanett, L. (1993). To walk in two worlds—or more? Challenging a common metaphor of native education. *Anthropology and Education Quarterly, 24*(2), 116–134.

Heshusius, L. (1982). At the heart of the advocacy dilemma. *Exceptional Children, 49,* 6–13.

Hines, P.M., & Boyd-Franklin, N. (1996). African American families. In M. McGoldrick, J. Giordano, & J.K. Pearce (Eds.), *Ethnicity and family therapy* (2nd ed., pp. 66–84). New York: Guilford Press.

Hinkle, J.S. (1994). Practitioners and cross-cultural assessment: A practical guide to information and training. *Measurement and Evaluation in Counseling and Development, 27,* 103–115.

Hmong family prevents surgery on son. (1991, January). *Omaha World Herald,* p. 16.

Ho, M.K. (1987). *Family therapy with ethnic minorities.* Thousand Oaks, CA: Sage Publications.

Hoberman, S., & Mailick, S. (Eds.). (1994). *Professional education in the United States: Experiential learning, issues, and prospects.* Westport, CT: Praeger.

Hodges, V.G., Burwell, Y., & Ortega, D. (1998). Empowering families. In L.M. Gutiérrez, R.J. Parsons, & E.O. Cox (Eds.), *Empowerment in social work practice: A sourcebook* (pp. 146–162). Pacific Grove, CA: Brooks/Cole.

Holdsworth, N. (1995, May 19). "Culture of dignity" for special needs. *Times Educational Supplement,* p. 14.

Hong, G.K., & Hong, L.K. (1991). Comparative perspectives on child abuse and neglect: Chinese versus Hispanics and Whites. *Child Welfare, 70*(4), 463–475.

Howing, P.T., & Wodarski, J.S. (1992). Legal requisites for social workers in child abuse and neglect situations. *Social Work, 27*(4), 330–336.

Hunter, B. (1982). Policy issues in special education for migrant students. *Exceptional Children, 48*(6), 469–472.

Illich, I. (1971). *Deschooling society.* New York: Harper & Row.

Individuals with Disabilities Education Act (IDEA) of 1990, PL 101-476, 20 U.S.C. §§ 1400 *et seq.*

Individuals with Disabilities Education Act Amendments of 1997, PL 105-17, 20 U.S.C. §§ 1400 *et seq.*

Ingstad, B. (1995). Mpho ya modimo—a gift from God: Perspectives on "attitudes" toward disabled persons. In B. Ingstad & S.R. Whyte (Eds.), *Disability and culture* (pp. 246–266). Berkeley: University of California Press.

Ishisaka, H.A., Nguyen, Q.T., & Okimoto, J.T. (1985). The role of culture in the mental health of Indochinese refugees. In T.C. Owan (Ed.), *Southeast Asian mental health: Treatment, prevention, services, training, and research* (pp. 41–63). Washington, DC: U.S. Department of Health and Human Services, National Institute of Mental Health.

Jablow, M.M. (1992). Introduction. In P.S. Buck, *The child who never grew* (2nd ed., pp. 1–23). Rockville, MD: Woodbine House.

Jacob, E. (1995). Reflective practice and anthropology in culturally diverse classrooms. *Elementary School Journal, 95,* 451–463.

Jalali, B. (1996). Iranian families. In M. McGoldrick, J. Giordano, & J.K. Pearce (Eds.), *Ethnicity and family therapy* (2nd ed., pp. 347–366). New York: Guilford Press.

James, A. (1995). Assessment with Native American families. *Family Resource Coalition Report, 14*(3 & 4), 19–20.

Janko, S. (1994). *Vulnerable children, vulnerable families: The social construction of child abuse.* Thousand Oaks, CA: Sage Publications.

Joe, J.R. (1997). American Indian children with disabilities: The impact of culture on health and education services. *Families, Systems, and Health, 15,* 251–261.

Kalyanpur, M. (1995, October). Developing cultural competence: Social skills training for classroom teachers of culturally diverse learners. *Social Skills Newsletter,* 2–5.

Kalyanpur, M. (1996). The influence of Western special education on community-based services in India. *Disability and Society, 11*(2), 249–270.

Kalyanpur, M. (1998). The challenge of cultural blindness: Implications for family-focused service delivery. *Journal of Child and Family Studies, 7*(3), 317–332.

Kalyanpur, M., & Harry, B. (1997). A posture of reciprocity: A practical approach to collaboration between professionals and parents of culturally diverse backgrounds. *Journal of Child and Family Studies, 6,* 487–509.

Kalyanpur, M., & Rao, S.S. (1991). Empowering low-income black families of handicapped children. *American Journal of Orthopsychiatry, 61,* 523–532.

Kao, R.S.-K., & Lam, M.L. (1997). Asian American elderly. In E. Lee (Ed.), *Working with Asian Americans: A guide for clinicians* (pp. 208–226). New York: Guilford Press.

Kim, B.-L. (1996). Korean families. In M. McGoldrick, J. Giordano, & J.K. Pearce (Eds.), *Ethnicity and family therapy* (2nd ed., pp. 281–294). New York: Guilford Press.

Kindermann, T., & Valsiner, J. (1989). Research strategies in culture-inclusive developmental psychology. In J. Valsiner (Ed.), *Child development in cultural context* (pp. 13–50). Toronto, Ontario, Canada: Hogrefe and Huber.

Kleinman, A. (1980). *Patients and healers in the context of culture.* Berkeley: University of California Press.

Korin, E.C. (1996). Brazilian families. In M. McGoldrick, J. Giordano, & J.K. Pearce (Eds.), *Ethnicity and family therapy* (2nd ed., pp. 200–213). New York: Guilford Press.

Ladson-Billings, G. (1994). *The dreamkeepers: Successful teachers of African-American children.* San Francisco: Jossey-Bass.

Laosa, L.M. (1983). Parent education, cultural pluralism, and public policy: The uncertain connection. In R. Haskins & D. Adams (Eds.), *Parent education and public policy* (pp. 331–345). Norwood, NJ: Ablex.

Lareau, A., & Shumar, W. (1996). The problem of individualism in family–school policies. *Sociology of Education, 69*(Suppl.), 24–39.

Lee, E. (1996). Asian American families: An overview. In M. McGoldrick, J. Giordano, & J.K. Pearce (Eds.), *Ethnicity and family therapy* (2nd ed., pp. 227–248). New York: Guilford Press.

Lehr, S., & Taylor, S.J. (1986). *Roots and wings: A manual about self-advocacy.* Boston: Federation for Special Needs.

Leon, E. (1996, September 7). *Challenges and solutions for educating migrant students.* Lansing: Michigan Department of Education. (ERIC Document Reproduction Service No. ED 393 615)

Leung, E.K. (1988, October). *Cultural and acculturational commonalities and diversities among Asian Americans: Identification and programming considerations.* Paper presented at the Ethnic and Multicultural Symposium, Dallas, TX. (ERIC Document Reproduction Service No. ED 298 780)

Leung, P.K., & Boehnlein, J. (1996). Vietnamese families. In M. McGoldrick, J. Giordano, & J.K. Pearce (Eds.), *Ethnicity and family therapy* (2nd ed., pp. 295–306). New York: Guilford Press.

Levin, H. (1990). At risk students in a yuppie age. *Educational Policy, 4,* 284–285.

Levy, R.I. (1996). Essential contrasts: Differences in parental ideas about learners and teaching in Tahiti and Nepal. In S. Harkness & C.M. Super (Eds.), *Parents' cultural belief systems: Their origins, expressions, and consequences* (pp. 123–142). New York: Guilford Press.

Lieberman, A.F. (1990). Infant–parent intervention with recent immigrants: Reflections on a study with Latino families. *Zero to Three, 10*(4), 8–11.

Lightfoot, S.L. (1978). *Worlds apart: Relationships between families and schools.* New York: Basic Books.

Lipka, J. (1991). Toward a culturally based pedagogy: A case study of one Yup'ik Eskimo teacher. *Anthropology and Education Quarterly, 22,* 203–223.

Livingston, S. (1997). *Rethinking the education of deaf students: Theory and practice from a teacher's perspective.* Portsmouth, NH: Heinemann.

Locust, C. (1988). Wounding the spirit: Discrimination and traditional American Indian belief systems. *Harvard Educational Review, 58,* 315–330.

Logan, S.L. (1996). A strengths perspective on Black families: Then and now. In S.L. Logan (Ed.), *The Black family: Strengths, self-help, and positive change* (pp. 8–20). Boulder, CO: Westview Press.

Lustig, M.W., & Koester, J. (1993). *Intercultural competence: Interpersonal communication across cultures.* New York: HarperCollins.

Lynch, E.W., & Hanson, M.J. (Eds.). (1998). *Developing cross-cultural competence: A guide to working with children and their families* (2nd ed.). Baltimore: Paul H. Brookes Publishing Co.

Lynch, E.W., & Stein, R. (1987). Parent participation by ethnicity: A comparison of Hispanic, Black, and Anglo families. *Exceptional Children, 54,* 105–111.

Magnussen, T. (1997). Marginalised young men and successful young women? Rural young people entering adulthood. In J. Wheelock & Å. Mariussen (Eds.), *Households, work, and economic change: A comparative institutional perspective* (pp. 187–194). Boston: Kluwer Academic.

Mahoney, K.S. (1995). School personnel and mandated reporting of child maltreatment. *Journal of Law and Education, 24*(2), 227–239.

Mallory, B.L. (1995). The role of social policy in life-cycle transitions. *Exceptional Children, 62,* 213–233.

Mardiros, M. (1989). Conception of childhood disability among Mexican-American parents. *Medical Anthropology, 12,* 55–68.

Margonis, F. (1992). The cooptation of "at risk": Paradoxes of policy criticism. *Teachers College Record, 94,* 343–364.

Marion, R. (1979). Minority parent involvement in the IEP process: A systematic model approach. *Focus on Exceptional Children, 10*(8), 1–16.

Markey, U.A. (1997). Valuing all families. *Tapestry: Weaving Sustaining Threads, 1*(3), 1. [Available from Grassroots Consortium on Disabilities, Post Office Box 61628, Houston, TX 77208.]

Marshall, C., Mitchell, D., & Wirt, F. (1989). *Culture and education policy in the American states.* New York: Falmer Press.

Maruyama, M. (1983). Cross-cultural perspectives on social and community change. In E. Seidman (Ed.), *Handbook of social intervention* (pp. 33–47). Thousand Oaks, CA: Sage Publications.

Matsui, W.T. (1996). Japanese families. In M. McGoldrick, J. Giordano, & J.K. Pearce (Eds.), *Ethnicity and family therapy* (2nd ed., pp. 268–280). New York: Guilford Press.

Matuszewski, J. (1996). Helping Tom learn to do for himself . . . with help. In L.E. Powers, G.H.S. Singer, & J.-A. Sowers (Eds.), *On the road to autonomy: Promoting self-competence in children and youth with disabilities* (pp. 189–193). Baltimore: Paul H. Brookes Publishing Co.

Maurice, C. (1994). *Let me hear your voice: A family's triumph over autism.* New York: Fawcett Books.

McCarty, T.L., Lynch, R.H., Wallace, S., & Benally, A. (1991). Classroom inquiry and Navajo learning styles: A call for reassessment. *Anthropology and Education Quarterly, 22,* 42–59.

McDermott, R., & Varenne, H. (1995). Culture *as* disability. *Anthropology and Education Quarterly, 26,* 324–348.

McDonnell, L.M., McLaughlin, M.J., & Morison, P. (Eds.). (1997). *Educating one and all: Students with disabilities and standards-based reform.* Washington, DC: National Academy Press.

McGillicuddy-De Lisi, A.V., & Subramanian, S. (1996). How do children develop knowledge? Beliefs of Tanzanian and American mothers. In S. Harkness & C.M. Super (Eds.), *Parents' cultural belief systems: Their origins, expressions, and consequences* (pp. 143–168). New York: Guilford Press.

McGoldrick, M., Pearce, J.K., & Giordano, J. (Eds.). (1996). *Ethnicity and family therapy* (2nd ed.). New York: Guilford Press.

McGowan, B.G. (1988). Helping Puerto Rican families at risk: Responsive use of time, space, and relationships. In C. Jacobs & D.D. Bowles (Eds.), *Ethnicity and race: Critical concepts in social work* (pp. 48–70). Silver Spring, MD: National Association of Social Workers.

McKenzie-Pollock, L. (1996). Cambodian families. In M. McGoldrick, J. Giordano, & J.K. Pearce (Eds.), *Ethnicity and family therapy* (2nd ed., pp. 307–315). New York: Guilford Press.

Mehan, H. (1988). Educational handicaps as a cultural meaning system. *Ethos: Journal of the Society for Psychological Anthropology, 16*(1), 73–91.

Mehan, H. (1993). Beneath the skin and between the ears: A case study in the politics of representation. In S. Chaiklin & J. Lave (Eds.), *Understanding practice: Perspectives on activity and context* (pp. 241–267). New York: Cambridge University Press.

Mehan, H., Hartwick, A., & Miehls, J.L. (1986). *Handicapping the handicapped: Decision-making in students' educational careers*. Stanford, CA: Stanford University Press.

Mehta, V. (1972). *Daddyji*. New York: Farrar, Strauss, & Giroux.

Mercer, C.D. (1997). *Students with learning disabilities*. Upper Saddle River, NJ: Merrill/Prentice-Hall.

Mercer, J. (1973). *Labeling the mentally retarded*. Berkeley: University of California Press.

Meyers, C. (1992). Hmong children and their families: Consideration of cultural influences on assessment. *The American Journal of Occupational Therapy, 46,* 737–744.

Miles, M. (1981). *A short circuit of mental handicap in India with some sparks of development*. Unpublished manuscript.

Miles, M. (1997). Disabled learners in South Asia: Lessons from the past for educational exporters. *International Journal of Disability, Development, and Education, 44,* 97–104.

Miles, M., & Miles, C. (1993). Education and disability in cross-cultural perspective: Pakistan. In S.J. Peters (Ed.), *Education and disability in cross-cultural perspective* (pp. 167–235). New York: Garland.

Miller, A.B., & Keys, C.B. (1996). Awareness, action, and collaboration: How the self-advocacy movement is empowering for persons with developmental disabilities. *Mental Retardation, 34,* 312–319.

Mlawer, M.A. (1993). Who should fight? Parents and the advocacy expectation. *Journal of Disability Policy Studies, 4*(1), 105–115.

Mohan, B. (1992). Trans-ethnic adolescence, confluence, and conflict: An Asian Indian paradox. In S.M. Furuto, R. Biswas, D.K. Chung, K. Murase, & F. Ross-Sheriff (Eds.), *Social work practice with Asian Americans* (pp. 189–201). Thousand Oaks, CA: Sage Publications.

Monks, J., & Frankenberg, R. (1995). Being ill and being me: Self, body and time in multiple sclerosis narratives. In B. Ingstad & S.R. Whyte (Eds.), *Disability and culture* (pp. 107–136). Berkeley: University of California Press.

Montessori, M. (1965). *Dr. Montessori's own handbook*. New York: Schocken.

National Commission on Children. (1991). *Beyond rhetoric: A new American agenda for families.* Washington, DC: Author.

Nicolaisen, I. (1995). Persons and nonpersons: Disability and personhood among the Punan Bah of central Borneo. In B. Ingstad & S.R. Whyte (Eds.), *Disability and culture* (pp. 38–55). Berkeley: University of California Press.

Ogbu, J.U. (1987). *Minority education and caste: The American system in cross-cultural perspective.* San Francisco: Academic Press.

Oughton, E., Wheelock, J., & Wiborg, A. (1997). Behind the lace curtains. In J. Wheelock & Å. Mariussen (Eds.), *Households, work, and economic change: A comparative institutional perspective* (pp. 37–52). Boston: Kluwer Academic.

Pacer Center [Producer]. (1992a). *Our children, our hopes* [Videotape]. Minneapolis, MN: Producer.

Pacer Center [Producer]. (1992b). Our family, our child [Videotape]. Minneapolis, MN: Producer.

Park, C.C. (1982). *The siege: The first eight years of an autistic child.* Boston: Back Bay Books/Little, Brown.

Pedersen, P.B. (1981). Alternative futures for cross-cultural counseling and psychotherapy. In A.J. Marsella & P.B. Pedersen (Eds.), *Cross-cultural counseling and psychotherapy* (pp. 312–337). New York: Pergamon.

Peisner, E.S. (1989). To spare or not to spare the rod: A cultural-historical view of child discipline. In J. Valsiner (Ed.), *Child development in cultural context* (pp. 111–144). Toronto, Ontario, Canada: Hogrefe and Huber.

Peterson, P.E., & Noyes, C. (1997). School choice in Milwaukee. In D. Ravitch & J.P. Viteritti (Eds.), *New schools for a new century: The redesign of urban education* (pp. 123–146). New Haven, CT: Yale University Press.

Philips, S. (1983). *The invisible culture: Cultural democracy, bicognitive development, and education.* New York: Academic Press.

Piercy, F., Soekandar, A., & Limansubroto, C.D.M. (1996). Indonesian families. In M. McGoldrick, J. Giordano, & J.K. Pearce (Eds.), *Ethnicity and family therapy* (2nd ed., pp. 316–323). New York: Guilford Press.

Piestrup, A.M. (1973). *Black dialect interference and accommodations of reading instruction in first grade.* Berkeley: University of California Press. (ERIC Document Reproduction Service No. ED 119 113)

Powers, L.E., Singer, G.H.S., & Sowers, J.-A. (1996). Self-competence and disability. In L.E. Powers, G.H.S. Singer, & J.-A. Sowers (Eds.), *On the road to autonomy: Promoting self-competence in children and youth with disabilities* (pp. 3–24). Baltimore: Paul H. Brookes Publishing Co.

Pyecha, J.N., & Ward, L.A. (1982). A study of the implementation of P.L. 94-142 for handicapped migrant children. *Exceptional Children, 48*(6), 490–495.

Racino, J.A., & Taylor, S.J. (1993). "People first": Approaches to housing and support. In J.A. Racino, P. Walker, S. O'Connor, & S.J. Taylor (Eds.), *Housing, support, and community: Choices and strategies for adults with disabilities* (Vol. 2, pp. 33–56). Baltimore: Paul H. Brookes Publishing Co.

Ramírez, M., & Casteñeda, A. (1974). *Cultural democracy, bicognitive development, and education.* New York: Academic Press.

Rao, S.S. (1996). *"A little inconvenience": Perspectives of Bengali families of children with disabilities on inclusion and disability.* Unpublished doctoral dissertation, Syracuse University.

Rauscher, L., & McClintock, M. (1997). Ableism curriculum design. In M. Adams, L.A. Bell, & P. Griffin (Eds.), *Teaching diversity and social justice: A sourcebook* (pp. 198–230). New York: Routledge.

Ravitch, D. (1997). Somebody's children: Educational opportunity for all of America's children. In D. Ravitch & J.P. Viteritti (Eds.), *New schools for a new century: The redesign of urban education* (pp. 251–274). New Haven, CT: Yale University Press.

Red Horse, J. (1998). American Indian elders: Unifiers of Indian families. *Social Casework, 61,* 490–493.

Reid, B.V.S. (1989). Socialization for moral reasoning: Maternal strategies of Samoans and Europeans in New Zealand. In J. Valsiner (Ed.), *Child development in cultural context* (pp. 193–222). Toronto, Ontario, Canada: Hogrefe and Huber.

Renz-Beaulaurier, R. (1998). Empowering people with disabilities: The role of choice. In L.M. Gutiérrez, R.J. Parsons, & E.O. Cox (Eds.), *Empowerment in social work practice: A sourcebook* (pp. 73–82). Pacific Grove, CA: Brooks/Cole.

Repetto, J.B., & Correa, V.I. (1996). Expanding views on transition. *Exceptional Children, 62,* 551–563.

Rhodes, R.L. (1996). Beyond our borders: Spanish-dominant migrant parents and the IEP process. *Rural Special Education Quarterly, 15*(2), 19–22.

Rogers-Dulan, J., & Blacher, J. (1995). African American families, religion, and disability: A conceptual framework. *Mental Retardation, 33,* 226–238.

Roit, M.L., & Prohl, W. (1984). The readability of P.L. 94-142 parent materials: Are parents truly informed? *Exceptional Children, 40,* 496–505.

Roseberry-McKibbin, C. (1995). Distinguishing language differences. *Multicultural Education, 2*(4), 12–16.

Ross-Sheriff, F. (1992). Adaptation and integration into American society: Major issues affecting Asian Americans. In S.M. Furuto, R. Biswas, D.K. Chung, K. Murase, & F. Ross-Sheriff (Eds.), *Social work practice with Asian Americans* (pp. 45–64). Thousand Oaks, CA: Sage Publications.

Scheer, J., & Groce, N. (1988). Impairment as a human constant: Cross-cultural and historical perspectives on variation. *Journal of Social Issues, 44,* 23–37.

Schön, D.A. (1983). *The reflective practitioner: How professionals think in action.* New York: Basic Books.

Schweder, R.A., Mahapatra, M., & Miller, J.G. (1990). Culture and moral development. In J.W. Stigler, R.A. Schweder, & G. Herdt (Eds.), *Cultural psychology: Essays on comparative human development* (pp. 134–203). Cambridge, England: Cambridge University Press.

Serpell, R. (1994). The cultural construction of intelligence. In W.J. Lonner & R.S. Malpass (Eds.), *Readings in psychology and culture* (pp. 157–163). Needham Heights, MA: Allyn & Bacon.

Serpell, R. (1997). Critical issues, literacy connections between school and home: How should we evaluate them? *Journal of Literacy Research, 29,* 587–616.

Serpell, R., Mariga, K., & Harvey, K. (1993). Mental retardation in African countries: Conceptualization, services, and research. *International Review of Research in Mental Retardation, 19,* 1–39.

Shafer, M.S., & Rangasamy, R. (1995). Transition and Native American youth: A follow-up study of school leavers on the Fort Apache Indian Reservation. *Journal of Rehabilitation, 61*(1), 60–65.

Shapiro, J., & Simonsen, D. (1994). Educational/support group for Latino families of children with Down syndrome. *Mental Retardation, 32,* 403–415.

Shwalb, D.W., Shwalb, B.J., & Shoji, J. (1996). Japanese mothers' ideas about infants and temperament. In S. Harkness & C.M. Super (Eds.), *Parents' cultural belief systems: Their origins, expressions, and consequences* (pp. 169–191). New York: Guilford Press.

Simon, J.P. (1996). Lebanese families. In M. McGoldrick, J. Giordano, & J.K. Pearce (Eds.), *Ethnicity and family therapy* (2nd ed., pp. 364–375). New York: Guilford Press.

Simpson, R.L. (1996). *Working with parents and families of exceptional children and youth: Techniques for successful conferencing and collaboration* (3rd ed.). Austin, TX: PRO-ED.

Skinner, D. (1989). The socialization of gender identity. In J. Valsiner (Ed.), *Child development in cultural context* (pp. 181–192). Toronto, Ontario, Canada: Hogrefe and Huber.

Skrtic, T.M. (1991). *Behind special education: A critical analysis of professional culture and school organization.* Denver: Love Publishing.

Skrtic, T.M. (1995a). The crisis in professional knowledge. In E.L. Meyen & T.M. Skrtic (Eds.), *Special education and student disability: An introduction. Traditional, emerging, and alternative perspectives* (4th ed., pp. 567–608). Denver: Love Publishing.

Skrtic, T.M. (1995b). Deconstructing/reconstructing the professions. In T.M. Skrtic (Ed.), *Disability and democracy: Reconstructing (special) education for postmodernity* (pp. 3–62). New York: Teachers College Press.

Skrtic, T.M. (1995c). The special education knowledge tradition: Crisis and opportunity. In E.L. Meyen & T.M. Skrtic (Eds.), *Special education and student disability: An introduction. Traditional, emerging, and alternative perspectives* (pp. 609–674). Denver: Love Publishing.

Sleeter, C. (1986). Learning disabilities: The social construction of a special education category. *Exceptional Children, 53,* 46–54.

Smart, J.F., & Smart, D.W. (1991). Acceptance of disability and the Mexican American culture. *Rehabilitation Counseling Bulletin, 34,* 357–367.

Smith, H.Y. (1996). Building on the strengths of Black families: Self-help and empowerment. In S.L. Logan (Ed.), *The Black family: Strengths, self-help, and positive change* (pp. 21–38). Boulder, CO: Westview Press.

Smith, M.J., & Ryan, A.S. (1987). Chinese-American families of children with developmental disabilities: An exploratory study of reactions to service providers. *Mental Retardation, 25,* 345–350.

Song-Kim, Y.I. (1992). Battered Korean women in urban United States. In S.M. Furuto, R. Biswas, D.K. Chung, K. Murase, & F. Ross-Sheriff (Eds.), *Social work practice with Asian Americans* (pp. 213–226). Thousand Oaks, CA: Sage Publications.

Sparrow, S., Balla, D., & Cicchetti, D. (1984). *Vineland Adaptive Behavior Scales.* Circle Pines, MN: American Guidance Service.

Spindler, F., & Spindler, L. (1990). *The American cultural dialogue and its transmission.* London: Falmer Press.

Stahl, A. (1991, December). Beliefs of Jewish-Oriental mothers regarding children who are mentally retarded. *Education and Training in Mental Retardation,* 361–369.

Sudarkasa, N. (1981). Interpreting the African heritage in Afro-American family organization. In H.P. McAdoo (Ed.), *Black families* (pp. 23–36). Thousand Oaks, CA: Sage Publications.

Sue, D.W., & Sue, D. (1990). *Counseling the culturally different: Theory and practice.* New York: John Wiley & Sons.

Super, C.M., & Harkness, S. (1986). The developmental niche: A conceptualization at the interface of child and culture. *International Journal of Behavioral Development, 9,* 545–569.

Sutton, C.T., & Broken Nose, M.A. (1996). American Indian families: An overview. In M. McGoldrick, J. Giordano, & J.K. Pearce (Eds.), *Ethnicity and family therapy* (2nd ed., pp. 31–44). New York: Guilford Press.

Swick, K.J. (1997). Involving families in the professional preparation of educators. *The Clearing House, 70,* 265–268.

Talle, A. (1995). A child is a child: Disability and equality among the Kenya Masai. In B. Ingstad & S.R. Whyte (Eds.), *Beyond culture* (pp. 56–72). Berkeley: University of California Press.

Taylor, S.J. (1988). Caught in the continuum: A critical analysis of the principle of the least restrictive environment. *Journal of The Association for Persons with Severe Handicaps, 13,* 41–53.

Tharp, R., & Gallimore, R. (1988). *Rousing minds to life: Teaching, learning, and schooling in social context.* New York: Cambridge University Press.

Tobin, J.J., Wu, D.Y.H., & Davidson, D.H. (1989). *Preschool in three cultures: Japan, China, and the United States.* New Haven, CT: Yale University Press.

Traustadottir, R. (1995). A mother's work is never done: Constructing a "normal" family life. In S.J. Taylor, R. Bogdan, & Z.M. Lutfiyya (Eds.), *The variety of community experience: Qualitative studies of family and community life* (pp. 47–66). Baltimore: Paul H. Brookes Publishing Co.

Trawick-Smith, J. (1997). *Early childhood development: A multicultural perspective.* Upper Saddle River, NJ: Merrill.

Trueba, H., Jacobs, L., & Kirton, E. (1990). *Cultural conflict and adaptation: The case of Hmong children in American society.* New York: Falmer.

Turbiville, V.P. (1994). *Fathers, their children, and disability.* Unpublished doctoral dissertation, University of Kansas, Lawrence.

Turnbull, A.P., & Ruef, M.B. (1996). Family perspectives on problem behavior. *Mental Retardation, 34,* 280–293.

Turnbull, A.P., & Turnbull, H.R. (1996). Self-determination within a culturally responsive family systems perspective: Balancing the family mobile. In L.E. Powers, G.H.S. Singer, & J.-A. Sowers (Eds.), *On the road to autonomy: Promoting self-competence in children and youth with disabilities* (pp. 195–220). Baltimore: Paul H. Brookes Publishing Co.

Turnbull, A.P., & Turnbull, H.R. (1997). *Families, professionals, and exceptionality: A special partnership* (3rd ed.). Upper Saddle River, NJ: Merrill/Prentice-Hall.

Turnbull, A.P., Turnbull, H.R., Shank, M., & Leal, D. (1999). *Exceptional lives: Special education in today's schools* (2nd ed.). Upper Saddle River, NJ: Merrill/Prentice-Hall.

Turnbull, H.R., & Turnbull, A.P. (with Buchele-Ash, A., & Rainbolt, K.). (1998). *Free appropriate public education: The law and children with disabilities* (5th ed.). Denver: Love Publishing.

Tyack, D.B. (1993). Constructing difference: Historical reflections on schooling and social diversity. *Teachers College Record, 95,* 8–34.

Tyack, D.B., & Hansot, E. (1982). *Managers of virtue: Public school leadership in America, 1820–1980.* New York: Basic Books.

U.S. Department of Labor. (1965). *The Negro family: The case for national action.* Washington, DC: U.S. Government Printing Office.

Valdés, G. (1996). *Con respeto: Bridging the distances between culturally diverse families and schools: An ethnographic portrait.* New York: Teachers College Press.

Vallance, E. (1983). Hiding the hidden curriculum: An interpretation of the language of justification in nineteenth-century educational reform. In H.A. Giroux & D. Purpel (Eds.), *The hidden curriculum and moral education: Deception or discovery?* (pp. 9–27). Berkeley, CA: McCutchan.

Valsiner, J. (1989a). How can developmental psychology become "culture-inclusive"? In J. Valsiner (Ed.), *Child development in cultural context* (pp. 1–10). Toronto, Ontario, Canada: Hogrefe and Huber.

Valsiner, J. (1989b). Organization of children's social development in polygamic families. In J. Valsiner (Ed.), *Child development in cultural context* (pp. 67–86). Toronto, Ontario, Canada: Hogrefe and Huber.

Walker, S. (1986). Attitudes toward the disabled as reflected in social mores in Africa. In K. Marfo, S. Walker, & B. Charles (Eds.), *Childhood disability in developing countries: Issues in habilitation and special education* (pp. 239–249). New York: Praeger.

Ward, M.J. (1996). Coming of age in the age of self-determination: A historical and personal perspective. In D.J. Sands & M.L. Wehmeyer (Eds.), *Self-determination across the life span: Independence and choice for people with disabilities* (pp. 3–16). Baltimore: Paul H. Brookes Publishing Co.

Ware, L.P. (1994). Contextual barriers to collaboration. *Journal of Educational and Psychological Consultation, 5,* 339–357.

Wechsler, D. (1991). *Wechsler Intelligence Scale for Children* (3rd ed.). San Antonio, TX: The Psychological Corporation.

Weisner, T.S. (1993). Ethnographic and ecocultural perspectives on sibling relationships. In Z. Stoneman & P.W. Berman (Eds.), *The effects of mental retardation, disability, and illness on sibling relationships: Research issues and challenges* (pp. 51–83). Baltimore: Paul H. Brookes Publishing Co.

Weiss, B.D., & Coyne, C. (1997). Communicating with patients who cannot read. *The New England Journal of Medicine, 337*(4), 272–274.

Welles-Nyström, B. (1996). Scenes from a marriage: Equality ideology in Swedish family policy, maternal ethnotherapies, and practice. In S. Harkness & C.M. Super (Eds.), *Parents' cultural belief systems: Their origins, expressions, and consequences* (pp. 192–214). New York: Guilford Press.

Whyte, S.R., & Ingstad, B. (1995). Disability and culture: An overview. In B. Ingstad & S.R. Whyte (Eds.), *Disability and culture* (pp. 3–35). Berkeley: University of California Press.

Wilson-Oyelaran, E.B. (1989). Towards contextual sensitivity in developmental psychology. In J. Valsiner (Ed.), *Child development in cultural context* (pp. 51–66). Toronto, Ontario, Canada: Hogrefe and Huber.

Wisconsin v. Yoder, 406 U.S. 205 (1972).

Wolfensberger, W. (1972). *Normalisation: The principle of normalisation in human services.* Toronto, Ontario, Canada: National Institute on Mental Retardation.

Wolfram, W. (with Detwyler, J., & Adger, C.). (1992). *All about dialects: Instructor's manual.* Washington, DC: Center for Applied Linguistics.

Wong, M.-H. (1989). Kohlberg's "just community" and the development of moral reasoning: A Chinese perspective. In J. Valsiner (Ed.), *Child development in cultural context* (pp. 87–110). Toronto, Ontario, Canada: Hogrefe and Huber.

Woodson, R.H., & da Costa, E. (1989). Features of infant social interaction in three cultures in Malaysia. In J. Valsiner (Ed.), *Child development in cultural context* (pp. 147–162). Toronto, Ontario, Canada: Hogrefe and Huber.

Wright, R., Saleeby, D., Watts, T.D., & Lecca, P.J. (1983). *Transcultural perspectives in the human services: Organizational issues and trends.* Springfield, IL: Charles C Thomas.

Ysseldyke, J.E., Algozzine, B., & Thurlow, M.L. (1992). *Critical issues in special education* (2nd ed.). Boston: Houghton Mifflin.

Zeitlin, M. (1996). My child is my crown: Yoruba parental theories and practices in early childhood. In S. Harkness & C.M. Super (Eds.), *Parents' cultural belief systems: Their origins, expressions, and consequences* (pp. 407–427). New York: Guilford Press.

Zinn, M.B., & Eitzen, D.S. (1993). *Diversity in families* (3rd ed.). New York: HarperCollins.

Zola, I.K. (1986). The medicalization of American society. In P. Conrad & R. Kern (Eds.), *The sociology of health and illness: Critical perspectives* (2nd ed., pp. 378–394). New York: St. Martin's Press.

Index

CPSIA information can be obtained at www.ICGtesting.com
Printed in the USA
LVOW061011180911

246781LV00004B/200/A

3 4711 00202 2780